# Letting Go
# of Worry

## DR. LINDA MINTLE

HARVEST HOUSE PUBLISHERS

EUGENE, OREGON

*Cover by Koechel Peterson & Associates, Inc., Minneapolis, Minnesota*

*Cover photo © iStockphoto / Thinkstock; back-cover author photo by Jim Whitmer*

Linda Mintle is published in association with Ambassador Literary Agency.

**LETTING GO OF WORRY**
Copyright © 2011 by Linda Mintle
Published by Harvest House Publishers
Eugene, Oregon 97402
www.harvesthousepublishers.com

Library of Congress Cataloging-in-Publication Data
Mintle, Linda.
Letting go of worry / Linda Mintle.
    p. cm.
ISBN 978-0-7369-3058-1 (pbk.)
ISBN 978-0-7369-4135-8 (eBook)
1. Worry—Religious aspects—Christianity. I. Title.
BV4908.5.M56 2011
248.8'6—dc22
                                                                2010050024

*To my family—*

*Through all the loss and difficult days,*
*thank you for concluding that despite what comes,*
*God is faithful.*
*I am grateful for such a rich heritage of faith.*

## Acknowledgments

Through our 36 years of marriage, you, Norm, have modeled what it means to allow faith to rule the day. You have led our family to the place we need to go when the cares of the world crowd our home. To my son, Matt, your ability to live in the moment challenges me to do more of the same. To my daughter, Katie, your joy is infectious and just your presence makes me smile. And to our dog Zoe, who patiently sat by my side during the writing of this book, thanks for prompting me to get up and take you for long walks! We both needed the regular breaks.

To my new family at Harvest House, thank you for waiting for me. LaRae, your persistence and encouraging conversations made this possible. Paul, thank you for being a kind and caring editor.

And finally…to God, who makes it possible to truly have a worry-free life.

# Contents

# Foreword

BY RUTH GRAHAM

My friend Dr. Linda Mintle has written a valuable book—it could be titled *All You Wanted to Know About Worry but Were Too Anxious to Ask*!

Does this sound like you?

If I pay the bills this month, I worry I won't have enough for next month.

If I did a good job on this project, I worry I won't meet expectations next time.

I worry that I won't fit into a new neighborhood.

I worry about what people will say or their opinion of me.

And if I don't have anything to worry about, I worry that I may be missing something!

Worry is my default position. I have beaten myself up over it for years. I blamed myself. I confessed it. I prayed about it. But round and round I'd go. And then I was asked to read the book you now hold in your hand, *Letting Go of Worry.*

Dr. Linda has given a readable and practical guide to understanding the "physiology" of worry. She gives insights that helped me see that worrying is an attempt to gain control of life's circumstances. It makes me think, falsely, that I am helping the situation, when in fact I am doing harm to myself. Worry does not prepare me for the future.

Dr. Linda gives us practical ideas we can use to help ourselves. You will find this book to be honest, down-to-earth, and always pointing to the truths we find in God and His Word. Dr. Linda shows us God's tools for letting go of worry—that if we apply them and not just skim over them, we will soon find worry's claws loosening their grip and contentment gaining ground.

Go ahead—buy this book. Read it and change your life as you let go of worry.

*Ruth Graham*

Introduction

# Take the Worry Challenge

In November 2006, the Kim family planned a fun trip over the Thanksgiving holiday. The family of four left their home in the Bay Area of California and headed for Seattle to be with family. On the way back to California via Interstate 5, they planned to turn off in southern Oregon and head toward the coastal town of Gold Beach, where they would stay in a hotel on the way back to San Francisco. But for some reason they never reached it. And when they failed to return to their home several days later, family and friends began to worry.

A missing persons report was filed, and the story was picked up by Bay Area news. Internet news sites followed the trail. There was no logical explanation for why the family had gone missing. The hotel in Gold Beach had never signed them in for the night. Despite their disappearance, hope was high that the family would be found.

As the story gained more public interest, the lives of James, his wife, Kati, and their two young daughters (ages seven months and four years) became known to the nation. Viewers and readers followed along as clues and details of the unfolding story were discovered.

A week went by, and still there was no sight of the family. It was as if the Kims had disappeared into nowhere. Search teams combed routes the family could have driven. With no specific leads and inclement weather, the search process was slow and arduous. The family's credit cards went unused, providing no clues to their whereabouts, but a pair of text messages sent to the Kims' phone would later prove useful.

The routes from Portland to Gold Beach include winding roads in high elevations. During the winter, the weather is changeable and often renders the roads impassable. Cell-phone coverage is spotty and most often fails. Piecing together details, using information regarding plans and reservations, and discovering the location of the cell tower used by the text messages, search teams narrowed the search to three possible routes. Private helicopters were hired by the extended family to assist police. Despite these daily efforts, no one was found. The relatives grew more fearful and frightened.

The search intensified. Nine days into the ordeal, Kati Kim and her two young daughters were spotted next to their Saab station wagon, waving a pink umbrella. Once they were aboard the chopper, rescue workers reported them to be in good condition. Considering they had been stranded on a back road in their car for days in snowy conditions, it was a miracle they were found alive. People rejoiced!

According to news reports, the family had taken a side road after missing their exit. The route was usually closed off in winter, but someone had vandalized the gate, leaving it open. As the road became impossible to travel because of the weather, the Kims parked their car for the night, hoping someone would find them in the morning.

Unfortunately, more snow fell, and they were stuck.

During the evenings, the family kept warm by running the car engine. When gas ran out, they burned the Saab's tires as a way to stay warm in the freezing temperatures. Melted snow became their source of water. Nearby a few berries were found to eat. Kati Kim used the little food they had and then nursed her daughters.

A number of days into the terrible ordeal, James Kim decided to go for help. He studied a map he had in the car and noticed a town he estimated to be about four miles away. The plan was to look for help. If unsuccessful, he would return by one o'clock in the afternoon. On a cold winter's morning, he kissed his family goodbye and began his trek into the unknown wilderness.

He never returned that day. But with the rescue of Kati and the girls, hope remained that he would be found.

The search for James led to a rugged canyon, where a pair of his pants was found. Rescuers believed he was wearing two pairs and might have used one to mark the return path. Others speculated that this could have been a sign of hypothermia because that condition leads to a feeling of being hot and would cause a person to shed their clothes. Given the uncertainty, hope prevailed that he was still alive.

As the search continued, more personal items and footprints were discovered. The evidence suggested that James had hiked three miles up the road but then found his way to a drainage area. It appeared as if he had tried to mark a path while he was walking.

Twelve days into the ordeal, the figure of James Kim was finally spotted in a rugged canyon. When rescuers made their way to the treacherous spot where his body lay, there was a glimmer of hope. A report came that he was talking. But hope was quickly replaced with despair. The information turned out to be incorrect.

Officials believed that James' journey had taken him more than ten miles in freezing conditions. The place his body was found was just a mile from the family car but separated by impassable terrain. And unbeknownst to him, a mile in another direction would have led him to a lodge closed for the winter but stocked with supplies. An autopsy later revealed that James Kim had died of hypothermia.

News of James' death spread rapidly through the media. Friends and strangers were deeply grieved by the tragic end to this story of hope and despair. Many had prayed for the family's safety. But despite heroic efforts by the extended Kim family and search-and-rescue squads, James' life ended in the cold and unfamiliar landscape of southern Oregon. When a sheriff's deputy broke the news of James' death, he dropped his head and cried. Everyone was deeply touched by this brave father who had tried to save his family, but met an untimely death at the age of 35.

One can only imagine the worry and anxiety experienced by family members during the days of not knowing the fate of James, Kati, and their daughters. As the country mourned, the sobering reality of life's uncertainty was felt in the hearts of those who had followed the story. As I read the accounts and posts written by people hanging on to hope that the family would be rescued, I thought about how quickly life can change. One day, the Kim family was celebrating Thanksgiving; the next, they were fighting for survival.

Each day, we do not know what tomorrow holds. And that uncertainty can drive us to a state of worry if we are not careful. And even if we are not lost on a mountain, there is plenty of uncertainty to create a daily dose of anxiety.

## A By-Product of Life's Uncertainty?

From the moment we are born, we experience feelings of vulnerability and powerlessness. We depend on others to take care of us and meet our basic needs of safety and love. If this does not happen, we feel anxious, and worry creeps in to our lives. And even when we are blessed with having our basic needs met, uncertainty is present. It is not possible to control all of our circumstances or know the future.

In the face of uncertainty, worry comes easily as a by-product. (I know because I come from a long line of worriers.) Our natural default is worry. And while most of us have not had to endure what the Kim family did, worry can still be invited in to our lives. Worry can accompany even the smallest of life's details. *How we handle life's uncertainty is what matters.*

Every day there are hundreds of opportunities to worry about something. Simply going about our daily routines provides us with ample worry material. I worry about being late and drinking too much coffee. Will my daughter be physically run down from her nonstop schedule? How do I get my son to make vegetables a food group in his diet? My husband refuses to use sunscreen even though his dad had skin cancer. My dog's eye condition is subject to change with age. *Pause. Take a deep breath. Think about your life.*

We worry about school safety, cavities at the dentist, making the soccer team, the late babysitter, and whether or not our boss will give us that deserved raise. Time and again we take normal situations of life and turn them in to worry moments. One unpleasant thing happens, and that is all it takes to kick worry into action.

And to everyday living we can add more serious worries like dealing with aging parents, losing a job, watching our 401K dwindle, or having a friend diagnosed with cancer. Difficult times bring more opportunities to pile on the worry.

Right now, for example, I am awaiting news of a friend who is going through brain surgery for tumor removal. I can worry about the tumor being malignant, the neurosurgeon making a wrong cut, the anesthesiologist dosing him too high, or even an unexpected problem developing on the operating table. Anything could go wrong. Then again, everything could go right. And the outcome has nothing to do with my worry. Somehow that doesn't stop most of us from shipping in a boatload of worry. In a crazy way, we believe worry helps us avoid a bad outcome.

When I want to add global problems to the worry mix, I simply turn on the television or read online news. Will we be safe from terrorists, suffer a flu epidemic, revive the economy, and stop the wrong people from acquiring nuclear weapons? Sometimes it is just too much information and makes my head spin. I'm not *24*'s Jack Bauer. I can't stop global mayhem. Yet seeing all the global disaster, my body gets aroused and my mind goes in to overdrive. News channels provide the perfect worry feast, and it doesn't take long at their tables. Another serving of world disorder, and I am ordering worry for dessert!

### Decide Where You Will Walk

We have become so accustomed to worry that we rarely consider why it has such power in our lives. It seems we have resigned ourselves to the fact that there is so little we can do about most things. Worry at least *feels* like we are doing something. Yet all we are doing is making ourselves miserable. Not the kind of *doing* we want!

Be honest. Do you want to live your life in a state of constant angst? Yet it seems we blindly accept worry as a normal part of being. For years I bought the idea that worry was unstoppable. I learned how to keep my anxious state manageable. I taught my clients to do the same.

But the more I look at the roots of worry and understand why it is so powerful, the more I realize it is wrong to accept worry as a life companion. Worry needs to be sent packing, not simply managed!

Although it may seem impossible, it is possible to be anxious about nothing and have true peace. Otherwise, the Bible would not give us such a directive. To do this means we have to stop justifying worry as part of modern living. Like me, you may need to rethink core beliefs. Why do I think worry has to live with me forever? Or maybe you need help capturing negative thoughts like, "What if…" You may lack trust about surrendering your worry to God. And that secret to contentment may be eluding you.

Allow me to challenge you to a worry-free life. I have accepted this challenge as I write this book. I have encountered many opportunities to apply what I am writing to you. And I promise you can learn to eliminate worry. When it creeps in, you can send it packing.

Right now, picture yourself with a quiet confidence that tells you, despite all of life's problems, that today and tomorrow will take care of themselves. Believe that contentment is an achievable goal. Together, let's look at the place worry occupies in our lives and decide if we want to give it space—any space at all!

**Start Saying Goodbye to Worry**

In regard to worry, we must learn to let go of what looks bad and trust the possible. A worry-free life can be ours even when circumstances are difficult. This was as true during the heart of the Depression as it is now. After Wall Street crashed in 1929, songwriter Dorothy Fields refused to give in to worry and wrote the optimistic lyrics of the song "On the Sunny Side of the Street."

During one of the gloomiest economic times in history, she penned a positive and optimistic message. Her upbeat challenge is to leave worry behind and get over to the sunny side of the street.

Decide where to walk. You can stay in the doom and gloom of your circumstances or hold on to hope and look at the bright side. The bright side is not that circumstances will always go your way, but rather that you are not alone in those circumstances. And as you face the many challenges this life presents, you can tolerate distress and work through those challenges worry free.

Problems come and go, but the decision to worry is something you can change. You can leave worry behind and not invite it back. You can walk on the sunny side of the street without living in denial. You have a choice to respond to life's uncertainty with worry and anxiety or with hope and confidence. Saying goodbye to worry is a decision you will not regret. It leads to a spacious, free life.

# Chapter I

# Everyone Worries, Don't They?

*There is a great difference between worry
and concern. A worried person sees a problem,
and a concerned person solves a problem.*

**HAROLD STEPHENS**

veryone worries, don't they? Maybe, but that does not mean it is good for us! At the risk of sounding like a mom, I'll say that just because everyone is doing it, does not mean *we* should. To believe *worry happens* and it cannot be stopped or controlled is wrong thinking! Our physical, emotional and spiritual health depends on dealing with worry the proper way.

You see, worry feeds on itself. It devours the soul and makes life miserable. It wastes a great deal of time and effort that could be applied elsewhere. Worry takes us down a negative path that typically ends in anxiety and distress, a path most of us want to avoid. And while we cannot change the facts associated with our worry, we can change our *decision* to worry. Worry invades our thoughts, but we decide if we will focus on it.

So the question is, is worry something we accept as a given and try to manage, or is it something from which we can be free? The answer is *yes*. Yes, we can learn to manage our worries. We can schedule a worry time each day, write down our worried thoughts, and do much more to manage it. Any therapist will tell you that worry can be managed. That is our job. We have an arsenal of tools that includes medications and behavioral strategies to help manage it. But is this the best we can do?

A better goal is to *rid* our lives of worry and learn to cultivate a life of peace and contentment. Personally, I am opting for a worry-free life, one that allows me to break away from the worry habit. Managing worry is too time-consuming and depressing. I have done it many times in my life. But from my faith perspective, managing worry is like managing adultery—both are just plain wrong and need to be stopped.

Like any habit, worry can be broken. To do so will take patience, intention, and understanding. We must pay attention to our bodies, examine our thinking, and look closely at our feelings. This means challenging the notion that worry simply happens and there is nothing we can do about it. There is much we can do about it, which is the focus of this book.

One of the reasons we hang on to worry is because it is easy to do. Worry helps us avoid the reality of the moment. It pulls our attention to an illusory world and allows us to disconnect for a short time. Although we may not be aware of it, a purpose is served when we worry. This is why it is so attractive.

In addition, most of us are good at worry. We have had many opportunities to practice. Worry has become a normal way of operating in our day-to-day living. It is like drinking our morning coffee, a habit we perform regularly without giving it much thought.

So here is the deal—you can worry and try to manage it, or you can choose to eliminate it from your life. The choice is yours. This book will focus on letting go of worry, not managing it. It will look at worry holistically and give you exercises at the end of each chapter to help you release it.

In order to say goodbye to worry, we begin by understanding the not-so-obvious but important difference between *concern* and *worry*. It is fine to be concerned about any number of issues, but not so fine to worry about them. Concern and worry are different.

## WHAT IS WORRY?

The word *worry* is related to the ancient German word *wur-gen*, meaning "to strangle." Now there is a pleasant thought.

Any word that has such a negative root cannot be good for us! Worry strangles the life out of us! It certainly feels that way when we worry. Worry is defined as "something or someone that causes anxiety; a source of unhappiness." It includes both how we feel and think.

The word's meaning has changed a bit through the centuries. Webster's 1828 dictionary defines worry as "to disturb, to tease, to harass, to weary." Today's Webster says to worry means to harass, to annoy, or to bother. As a noun, worry refers to a state of mind; anxiety; distress; care; uneasiness. In other words, worry involves a state of mind and engages our mental process, leading to anxious feelings or an anxious state.[1]

Thus, worry is a way to think, a mental habit. And this mental habit leads to feeling anxious. The focus of worry is typically future events where there is uncertainty about the outcome. To the worrier, the future is perceived as potentially negative, which creates feelings of anxiety.

Based on these definitions, are you beginning to see that worry is not associated with good things? Strangling, distress, disturbance, anxiety—not exactly the words we want to describe our behavior or thoughts! And certainly not words we associate with peace and calm.

## Lions, and tigers, and bears, oh my...

In the famous movie *The Wizard of Oz*, our heroine, Dorothy, cautiously proceeds down the yellow brick road searching for the Wizard, unsure of what she might encounter. Word is that lions, tigers and bears lurk in the dark of the forest, waiting to pounce on Dorothy and her companions. Concerned, Dorothy asks, "Do you suppose we'll meet any wild animals?" The Scarecrow answers, "Mm, we might. Animals that eat straw?" The Tin Woodman replies, "Some, but mostly lions, and tigers, and bears."

Dorothy, a stranger to the land, has no way of knowing how real or unreal the threat of attack is. She responds with her now famous "Lions, and tigers, and bears, oh my…" Was that an "oh my…" of concern or worry? What is the difference between being concerned versus worried?

Both concern and worry involve thinking, taking energy to focus on important issues. Yet they are distinctly different. Concern is normal and natural. In her travels, Dorothy does not know what to expect and is asking questions. She is in a strange land and making a long journey to an unknown destination. What might be on the road ahead?

Worry, on the other hand, is destructive, unhealthy, and misplaced. Worried thoughts focus on negativity and the what-ifs in life. Whereas concern moves us forward, worry keeps us stuck. Worry is the Scarecrow paralyzed by fear. He does not want to move on down the road—*what if* the animals eat straw?

Concern involves caring and meeting a need. Concern is the Tin Woodman reassuring the Scarecrow that while there might be wild animals that eat straw, it is unlikely, and there is a bigger goal—finding the Wizard. In other words, Scarecrow, it is not all about you and the slight possibility of being eaten. Stop looking for trouble and start thinking about finding the Wizard!

Concern comes out of a maturity and growth. It involves the ability to see reality, feel empathy or compassion, and care about others. Concern says, we are in the forest, let's take precautions but not lose our cool. Keep moving down the yellow brick road and solve problems when and if they materialize. Dorothy gets it, and she mobilizes the group to action.

Worry, on the other hand, is pointless and immobilizing. It circles the same problem with no real solution or control over what is happening. Most often it leads to anxiety.

In fact, worry causes more problems. It distracts from the goal, gets in the way of our destination, disrupts our plans, and creates havoc along the way. But concern prompts action that is in our control and works to solve the problem. It allows us to focus on a problem with the intent to do something about it.

Consider these comparisons between worry and concern. They will help you examine your thoughts and feelings:

| WORRY | CONCERN |
|---|---|
| Circles the problem | Solves the problem |
| Brings inaction | Brings action |
| Feels out of control | Takes control where possible |
| Distracts from the problem | Focuses on the problem |
| Disrupts a plan | Puts forth a plan |

### Concern is normal—worry needs to be eliminated

Once we understand the difference between concern and worry, it is freeing. It is normal to be concerned about life, people, and circumstances. We care about others and plan for the future. However, what we do with normal concerns is important. The temptation is to allow them to become times of worry. This example illustrates the difference between someone who is genuinely concerned and someone who is worried.

When Bill lost his job, he felt terrible. There were bills to pay and mouths to feed. Without an income, there would soon be a problem for his family. Instead of worrying about what could happen if he failed to find employment, Bill immediately applied for new positions. He updated his resume, worked his contacts, and stayed active and positive looking for a new job. His appropriate concern over losing his job spurred him on. He realized the consequences and took action. And that is what concern does—gets us to focus on the here and now and not be distracted by the negatives of a situation. Concern also helps us plan and move forward. It does not disrupt our plans or keep us stuck.

A worried Bill would have acted differently. Worried Bill would have been up all night, rehearsing the possibilities of debt while feeling paralyzed by fear. Mentally, he would be thinking about what he could have done to avoid losing his job. While this might have been productive if it had changed his behavior for future employment and brought clarity to his job loss, all worried Bill does is focus on those things he cannot control—the terrible job market, his age and ability to compete with younger colleagues, finding a salary commensurate with his experience, and so on. Panic sets in, and worried Bill believes there is too much working against him. He is immobilized by worry—stuck. Anxiety overtakes him, and he makes no moves forward.

When you are concerned, you live in the moment but do not ignore the realities of life. You see problems and challenges but keep moving forward. When you worry, you also see problems and challenges but get stuck in them. There is no moving forward.

## Concern does not need to become worry

So if our goal is to say goodbye to worry, how do we stop concern from morphing into worry? Is there a line between them? I believe so. And we must recognize when we have crossed that line.

To give an example, let's say you had a fight and your spouse threatened divorce (this is a no-no in marital fighting!). The fight was heated, but you eventually worked through it. Apologies were made. Your spouse insisted he did not mean the divorce comment. The heat of the moment led him to say hurtful things.

The next week, another conflict arises and, for a moment, you recall the last fight: "Maybe he does want a divorce..." But you do not dwell on that thought and decide to deal with the present conflict. Once again, the two of you work through the conflict. Nothing about divorce was mentioned this second time. But then you revisit the thoughts you had a fight ago: "Maybe he was thinking about divorce and did not say it. He probably wants out of the marriage. What else is he not telling me?"

Your thoughts have now moved from normal concern to worry. Your "mind-reading" is causing you to feel distressed and think your relationship is in trouble. Rather than ask about that past comment, you fret over what could be real or unreal. The mental gymnastics of worry begin!

Something negative from the past is not a problem as long as you do not dwell on it and assume it will repeat. Worry is created when negative thinking sticks around long after the fact.

So in the example above, there was concern about the divorce comment, but that comment was over and done, a thing of the past.

However, resurrecting the negative thought brought worry to the relationship.

Now, if you were bothered by the potential meaning of the divorce comment (was it careless, intended, a way to provoke, or something else?), then the proactive strategy would be to ask your spouse if he meant what he said, because it was hurtful and raised doubt in your mind. This is an action step and a way for you to take control over those potentially worrisome thoughts. With no move to action, the comment can take on a life of its own and turn to worry.

When we take apart the above example, we notice two things:

1. Something from the past was revisited and resurrected.

2. The negative was assumed, and the person operated in doubt instead of clarifying the comment (a problem-solving skill).

Concern moved to worry through revisiting the past and assuming the negative.

Here is another example. Jennifer noticed she was gaining weight. Her pants felt tight and she was eating when bored. Jennifer was concerned about the weight gain so she decided to make a behavioral change. When she felt bored, she worked crossword puzzles instead of eating. This activity distracted her. Concern about weight gain moved her to action and pushed her to make a plan and take control over an area of her behavior that felt out of control.

Jennifer could easily have moved her concern to worry. Here is how. She could focus her thoughts on how difficult it is to lose weight. After all, she has failed many diets and gained weight in the past. She could obsess on past dieting failures and also on how difficult it will be to break the current habit of eating when bored. What if she fails again? What if she does not lose weight? She will not be able to fit in her clothes. Her pants are already tight. This is depressing. Anxiety rises and she feels hopeless about doing anything. There is no moving forward because she is stuck in anxiety.

Basically, Jennifer is now circling the problem, becoming immobilized and doing no problem-solving. She allows distress to distract her from planning any helpful strategies. Her focus on past failures feeds worry.

Can we be concerned about events, issues, and people in our lives? Absolutely. Can we cry out to God about our concerns and feel deeply emotional? Certainly. King David did so regularly, as documented in the Psalms. Concern and catharsis are not worry. Worry goes beyond concern and catharsis and leads to a host of problems. In a word, worry looks backward and revisits failure and looks forward and assumes the worse.

**Fear, a close relative to worry**

Worry is often associated with fear. As with worry and concern, there is a difference between worry and fear. Consider this. If we are swimming in the warm Gulf waters and someone yells, "Shark!" fear is our natural response. Fear is a warning system built into our bodies as a natural reaction to danger. The danger is specific, timely, comes and goes quickly, and sharpens our senses. It is healthy to feel fear in the midst of a shark sighting. Fear acts like an alarm and often prompts us to action—in this case, swim as fast as you can and get out of the water!

Worry deals with what *might* happen and is a type of manufactured fear. So, for example, worry is when we again take a swim in the Gulf. There is no shark danger this time, but we worry that there could be. The entire time we swim, we feel anxious, thinking something bad could happen even though there is no evidence of it.

In this case, worry develops by thinking that danger could be hiding in those waters. In other words, worry takes fear and adds *what if*…to our thinking. Our thoughts move from the present reality to the possibility of danger. Although there is no present danger, we act and think as if there is. Worry remembers a time when a shark sighting happened and assumes it could happen right now. This resurrects fear.

Fear is often at the heart of worry. It motivates us to begin the *what if* cycle of worry. *What if* a shark is hiding? *What if* I get caught in the water? *What if* I cannot swim fast enough? *What if* no one sees me in trouble? And so on. Worry takes a real threat or a perceived danger (fear) and turns it into a way to focus on the uncertainty of the future:

You could get hit by a car, struck by lightning, lose your money in the stock market, and so on ad infinitum. While fear can be traced back to a specific event or experience, worry is vague and ill defined.

In an article for *Psychology Today*, psychiatrist Dr. Edward Hallowell, a former Harvard professor, described worry as "a special form of fear." He explained that simple fear becomes more complex once we add anticipation, memory, imagination, and emotion to the mix.[2] This "special form of fear" consumes both time and energy and threatens our mental and physical health. He was right. When you break down worry, fear is usually behind the scene. And that fear can translate to worry when we allow our thinking, emotions, and imagination to take us there.

## Worry and anxiety

You may also think that worry is not all that different from anxiety. I believe there is a difference, but it is a matter of degree and complexity. Anxiety has physical, mental, emotional, and behavioral components to it. When we are anxious, our heart races, palms sweat, blood pressure rises, and pupils dilate. Mentally, anxiety involves negative self-talk and negative automatic thoughts. Behaviorally, anxiety causes us to avoid or escape situations.

Worry could be thought of as the mental part of anxiety. It is a type of negative self-talk that promotes negative possibilities. It goes beyond normal thoughts of danger and threat and becomes a form of self-harassment that keeps us stuck and distressed.

Worry triggers anxiety arousal in the body. And when this arousal remains for a period of time, it can result in health problems, procrastination, relationship stress, and more. Like fear, chronic anxiety creates stress on the body and can get in the way of everyday living. On top of that, it steals our joy.

If unchecked, worry can lead to a host of anxiety-related disorders. When it becomes a way of life and involves multiple areas of living, it can develop into a *generalized anxiety disorder* (GAD). Health anxiety, or *hypochondria,* develops when benign body signs are interpreted as potential illness. Worry that takes the form of self-criticism, guilt, feelings of incompetence and helplessness, or pessimism can lead to *depression disorders*. Obsessive thoughts followed by compulsive behavior that is intrusive and frightening are what characterizes *obsessive-compulsive disorder* (OCD). Panic is felt when worry involves a loss of control and fear. After a trauma, worry about more danger and flashbacks of the trauma can develop into *posttraumatic stress disorder* (PTSD). Worry about embarrassment and social performance can intensify to a point of developing *social anxiety* or a *social phobia*. Finally, fear regarding an object or thing can turn in to a *specific phobia* like being afraid of dogs, spiders, or heights.

∞

Here is the challenge. Understand that your body reacts to normal situations of fear and anxiety, but do not allow fear or anxiety to linger, like a dysfunctional friend. Become aware of worried thoughts before they become a chronic problem that is fear-based or anxiety-producing. Know the difference between worry and concern, between fear and anxiety. Do not allow worry to lead you to a state of anxiety and fear. The rest of this book will help you to achieve these aims.

## Worry-Free Exercise

### BODY:

Check for physical tension. Do you have any of the physical signs of anxiety such as a racing or pounding heart, sweaty palms, difficulty breathing, stomach upset, frequent urination, diarrhea, muscle tension, headaches, fatigue, or insomnia? Be aware of your body and the physical sensations that creep in with stress, anxiety, fear, and worry.

### SOUL:

List your concerns—those things that bother you and could potentially become areas of worry. Using the table on page 21 (the differences between worry and concern), go through each concern and determine:

1. Is this a concern, or has it turned into a worry?

2. Is this concern something that is in or out of my control?

3. If it is in my control, what am I doing about it?

4. If it is not in my control, can I allow it to be that way without worrying?

Your goal is to empty this list by the end of the book.

## SPIRIT:

Take your concerns to God. Meditate on Deuteronomy 31:8:

> *The LORD himself goes before you*
> *and will be with you;*
> *he will never leave you nor forsake you.*
> *Do not be afraid; do not be discouraged.*

*Note*: If you feel you have excessive worry or worry to the point that it interferes with your everyday living, consider seeing a mental-health therapist trained in treating anxiety disorders. An evaluation can help determine if your worry has become anxiety. Anxiety disorders are treatable. There is help.

Chapter 2

# Life, Difficult Times, and the Nightly News

*Worrying is like a rocking chair—it gives you*
*something to do, but it gets you nowhere.*
—GLENN TURNER

L ife brings so many opportunities to worry that we may never stop to
consider what prompts us to do it. Actually, there are several con-
tributors to worry. Our biology, life circumstances, and experiences all
play a role. Because of this, saying goodbye to worry may be more difficult for some of us than others.

**Wired to worry?**

When it comes to worry, genetics play a role. Consider the difference between two teenagers preparing for a college exam. One teen
studied all night for her SAT and was a wreck the morning she sat for
the exam. Another teen reviewed the material the night before, went
to bed, and then calmly sat in the room and answered the questions.
What accounts for the difference? In this case it is biology. One teen is
more wired to worry than the other.

Here is another case in which genetics play a role. Two people get
ready to go to a party where most of the people attending will be strangers. One person sees this opportunity as exciting and a chance to meet
interesting people. The other person is worried sick—will she know
what to say, act confident, be able to make conversation or tolerate the
tension of meeting new people? What if she wears the wrong outfit,

makes a social faux pas, embarrasses herself, spills a drink, or something else? One person is energized by the uncertainty of the night; the other is almost paralyzed by it.

Both of the above examples illustrate the importance biology plays. Those born with a predisposition to anxiety (remember, worry is often tied to anxiety) have a genetic makeup that brings out the worrier in them. Science has proven that personality traits are encoded in our DNA. And those codes can predispose us to worry.

In 2007, Yale researchers found a gene variation associated with chronic worrying and what they call "overthinking." The "worry gene" is the result of a genetic mutation that predicts a tendency to ruminate (obsess over negative thoughts).[1] In fact, parts of the brain associated with planning, reason, and impulse control show increased activity in worriers.[2]

Areas of the brain are linked along a circuit. The way the brain is wired regulates our response to danger and threatening events. For some people, that circuitry is more activated and causes more anxiety and frustration. This is the case with people who are diagnosed with obsessive-compulsive disorder (OCD).

Swedish and German scientists also believe that two genes account for the development in some people of fears that are not easily overcome.[3] Without overwhelming you with science, the point is that our genetic makeup interacts with the environment, causing some of us to be more susceptible to fear and anxiety.

Knowing this should help you worry less about why you worry. Having said that, I do not want you to worry about your susceptibility to worry! For those of you who do possess these newly discovered anxiety genes, it still takes stressful life events to bring worry to the forefront. Having a tendency toward worry does not mean you will automatically become Chicken Little! But you may need to be more intentional about sending worry packing.

### Life circumstances and experiences

In addition to our genetic makeup, worry is something that can be learned over time in response to our environment. Life happens. An earthquake shakes a community; a family member is diagnosed with cancer; a son is sent to Afghanistan; a baby is born with heart problems. These difficult life experiences can bring worry to our lives. They shake up our normal routine and bring an awareness of uncertainty to everyday living. And when circumstances or difficult times shake our confidence, worry can be a natural response.

I noticed this immediately after 9/11. I was scheduled to fly a few days after the grounding of planes ended. As I boarded my plane, I sensed a different atmosphere among those flying that day. Passengers scrutinized every person who boarded in a way I had never seen. Those with a Mideastern physical appearance were especially watched. People were extra vigilant when seated, scoping out the behavior of others, watching them to see if there were any signs of unrest. Most looked anxious and were uncharacteristically quiet.

I sat next to a lady who was flying for the first time in her life, and she was terrified. The out of control events of 9/11 obviously heightened worry. People felt especially vulnerable because of the recent terrorist attacks. The atmosphere was filled with tension and uncertainty.

Negative life experiences make us more susceptible to worry because these experiences raise feelings of vulnerability and powerlessness. The more we experience those feelings and do not know what to do with them, the easier it is to worry.

So, for example, if you grew up in a home with an alcoholic parent, you experienced a great deal of unpredictability. One night your father might come home drunk and be pleasant—the next night, he might be mean. Day to day, you did not know what to expect. This unpredictability put you in a vulnerable and powerless position as a child.

The same is true if you experienced abuse or had family members with mental illness, addictions, and so on. The more vulnerable and powerless we feel, the more worry can be used as a false way to feel in control or avoid the reality of the present.

Any situation that feels out of control can trigger worry. I was reminded of this when watching preschoolers in a game in Sunday-school class at church. The teacher decided to have the children sit on balloons until they popped. They were not told the balloons would pop as they bounced on them. When the first one popped, a few of the children giggled with delight but others were terrified. The innocent game proved to be too much for those who were sensitive to loud sounds and startled by the popping. A few of the children were so shaken that they refused to return to the class the next week. They were worried and frightened. The game had felt out of control.

Everyday situations that are out of our control can trigger worry. A husband is late for dinner because of traffic, a woman spills coffee on her clothes at the drive-through and is late for work, a teen hears a comment about her appearance and is embarrassed, an employee is yelled at for no apparent reason, and so on. Whenever a situation feels out of our control, feelings of vulnerability or powerlessness result. One way to respond is to worry.

### SHARI'S EXPERIENCE

Shari got lost driving home from school and did not know what to do. She found herself in an unfamiliar part of town. She began to panic, realizing she was circling the same roads and not finding the highway she needed. That morning, she had left her cell phone by her bed, and she had no GPS or map in the car. Afraid she would run out of gas, she began to cry. She pulled over to the side of the road, too frightened to get out of her car. How would she get home? A wave of anxiety flooded her.

A police officer happened to see Shari sitting in her car and stopped to help. She eventually got home but felt that her ability to do so was based on a random event. Had it not been for the police officer, she would have been stranded. Her confidence was so shaken that every time she got in her car now, she was overwhelmed with anxiety. She worried to the point that she would not go anywhere that was unfamiliar. Nursing that feeling of vulnerability every time she entered her car led to a chronic worry habit.

Like Shari, we often face situations that feel out of control. Our ability to problem-solve and control our thoughts has everything to do with keeping worry at bay. When we do not handle a situation well, worry takes control if we allow it.

### Trauma on the slopes and in the not-so-friendly skies

Trauma can also set off worry. When actress Natasha Richardson died from an epidural hematoma following a skiing accident in Canada, a bump to the head took on heightened significance for skiers. Skiers fall on the slopes all the time, but they do not expect to die from those falls. When Richardson fell, she probably was not thinking death would be the outcome. But in some cases, head trauma can cause bleeding, bleeding that can lead to death. And that is what happened to Richardson—she died from the fall.

According to news reports, after Richardson fell, she showed no signs of physical injury. In fact, she joked, said she felt fine, and refused medical attention. This was one reason people were shocked when she died. She was one of those rare cases where the fall caused a fatal brain hemorrhage. The trauma of her death raised anxiety for some skiers. And anxiety from trauma creates worry for us if we are not careful.

My own story is an example of how worry can develop through trauma experiences. After seven years of infertility, a miscarriage, and several grueling medical procedures, I was finally pregnant. Overjoyed and feeling incredibly blessed, I approached the six-month mark of this pregnancy. And out of nowhere, panic seized me, leaving me paralyzed emotionally.

The sudden moments of terror and dread were recognizable because I had treated numerous patients with panic over the years. Even though I could manage the panic and eventually calm myself, I did not want to live this way. It made no sense. This pregnancy was something I had longed for and desperately wanted to happen. I was not going to allow anything to steal my joy for the last three months. So I began to search for answers.

Because of my clinical training and experience, I knew that *loss* is usually at the *root* of worry. It is not always easy to see the connection between worry and loss, but when you look hard enough, you can usually find it.

So I wondered, *Why was this happening to me now?* I was happy, even elated about the pregnancy. For the first time in seven years I was *not* thinking about loss, but life. I began to dig a little deeper. What about other times in my life when I had dealt with loss?

When I was ten years old, my mother was diagnosed with cancer. I did not really understand the seriousness of this disease. The fact that my mother could die was not something I thought about because she handled the cancer with amazing strength. Rarely did she miss work while going through radiation treatments. And she and my father did not talk about death, but steadily went about life as if the cancer was an inconvenience. Cancer was mentioned only when my grandparents came to the house to pray for my mom. Through prayer and sound medical treatment, my mom was healed and remained cancer-free for 40- plus years. The doctors said it was a miracle. To me, my mom's healing was a powerful sign that God existed and was taking care of us. Loss averted. No need to worry.

A few years later, a car hit my middle brother on his motorcycle. The crash put him into a coma with an uncertain prognosis. As I, then a high school student, stood by his bedside, his unmoving body was frightening—but again, my family turned to our faith. We prayed around my brother's bed for days, and he too was miraculously healed— another testimony to God's power and protection. What could have been a significant loss ended in celebration.

Despite the traumas, God intervened and the outcomes were positive. So when my older brother was drafted to fight in the Vietnam war, our family again prayed for protection. Because my brother was a college graduate, he was sent to officers' school so he could lead a platoon. His pregnant wife and their toddler remained in the States while he served his tour of duty in Vietnam. The day he arrived home was joyous—banners on the garage, a party, and a moving reunion. God kept his hand on my brother through that difficult war. Again, we were so blessed.

Months later, things changed dramatically.

It was the end of my senior year of high school. I was eagerly antic-ipating the future. I ended the year with high honors and had been accepted at the University of Michigan to study law.

Meanwhile, my family was preparing for my middle brother's wed-ding. During that time, my older brother, still an officer in the army, was asked to accompany a prestigious group of officers on a world tour related to his work in biology. He agonized over the trip because it would require missing my other brother's wedding. Our family took a vote and agreed that he could not pass up this career opportunity. It was too critical to his future. He should go on this seven-week tour.

My brother left on his trip and I enjoyed Michigan's warm summer days. One day in June I was arrived home from seeing my boyfriend. My father was in the house. Midday. Immediately I knew something was terribly wrong. In the kitchen, an army officer sat next to him delivering the news we never wanted to hear—my brother was miss-ing. His plane had gone down over New Delhi, India, and he had not survived.

Mom was at work. Dad called her home. He knew she could not handle this news over the phone. When she approached the back door and saw the officer sitting in our kitchen, she screamed, "My son is dead!" and fainted. A chill went down my back and I felt very alone, powerless to act. But there was no time to think, because my dad had to inform my brother's wife of her husband's death.

I am close to my father. He is a good man, steady, with quiet strength. The kind of humble man you can always depend on to do the right thing. I was to ride with him and my middle brother to deliver the news. My sister-in-law, pregnant with her second child, was visiting her mom with her two-year-old son. My job was to observe her when Dad deliv-ered the news. If she went into shock, I was to call 9-1-1.

When my dad explained my role, panic hit. "I am not a doctor. How will I know? What if she loses the baby? I can't do this. I don't want to do this." But there was no time to discuss details. Anxiety flooded me. We arrived at the house, though I have no recollection of that short trip. I do remember how the sun's rays poured through the living-room window, falling on the chair where my sister-in-law sat. When Dad told her what had happened, all I could think about was the state of the baby in her womb. She did not move or speak. I guessed she was in shock. I was emotionally paralyzed. The empty, yet terrified expression on her face was forever etched in my memory. Powerless to act, I just stood there.

Later we would receive the bloodied dog tags, a wallet, and my brother's briefcase. There was no body, no closure, no goodbye. The same God who had healed my mom from cancer and my brother from a coma, and protected my brother during Vietnam, allowed his plane to crash near a city in India. How could this be? The traumatic loss altered my life. And the panic I felt when I recalled this memory was the same panic I was now feeling years later, six months into my own pregnancy.

As I rehearsed the events of my brother's death, I suddenly realized something I had never seen before. It was obvious now, but I had overlooked it for years. My sister-in-law had been six months pregnant with her second child when my brother was killed. The same panic I had felt all those years ago when I had to give her the news of her husband's death was now paralyzing me in the present. Just like my sister-in-law, I was six months pregnant with my second child. I had not made this connection.

Up until then, every time my husband had traveled by plane for his job, I had been a basket case and had not understood why. Now I understood. Deep down, I was afraid my husband was going to die. I did not trust God. I was vulnerable and powerless to prevent bad things from happening.

Tears streamed down my face. I knew my thoughts about God were irrational, but I was struggling with them because of my experience. My head told me not to give up on God, but my heart was griped with anxiety. If I was honest, I did not trust God to protect me in the present. Over the years, I allowed what I saw as the injustice of my brother's death to grow to a point of unbelief—God could not be trusted.

My negative thoughts prompted feelings of fear, anxiety, and worry. If my brother could be killed when his wife was pregnant, so could my husband. I suddenly realized I was still that fearful girl, worried that God might fail to protect me. I falsely believed He had abandoned our family and me. These thoughts and my lack of trust had gripped me for years but had now come to the forefront with my pregnancy.

## Changing Our Responses

My story shows how worry is prompted by thoughts and beliefs. Sometimes we are not aware of what those thoughts and beliefs might be. They operate under cover and cause us to feel and act in ways that do not always seem rational. Other times, we know our thoughts and beliefs are negative, but succumb to them because we are hurt and afraid. The result is worry. Trauma can bring those worried thoughts to life.

Loss that is unexpected, traumatic, or difficult can lead to future worry if it is not grieved or handled well. Loss must be grieved, with full emotional expression—the layers of emotions and thoughts associated with it must be worked on through the years. Grieving is not easy because we do not like to feel the emotional pain that accompanies it. But it is the grieving process that leads to acceptance. It takes time and cannot be hurried. However, moving through the pain, rather than avoiding it, brings closure. When you face the pain, you realize you can tolerate it. But it hurts…and worry numbs the hurt.

Experiences of wounding and hurt are prime times for unbelief and doubt to creep in to our thoughts. So it is important to "take our thoughts captive" during grief. We will discuss this in a later chapter.

ತ

We cannot control bad things and prevent them from happening. But we can control how we emotionally respond to them. When we try to avoid, be strong, and not grieve our losses, we can easily get stuck. Grieving, feeling emotional pain, and learning to tolerate distress moves us forward.

Combining trauma, difficult life experiences, and genetics gives a potent cocktail for worry. Worry can be used like a barricade against perceived danger, but it does not do the job. Things happen despite our tendency to worry. Still, we can cling to worry and choose to see the world in a worried way, or allow our thoughts to wander into worried waters.

No matter what prompts worry, we can change. It is our response to trauma, the environment, situations, and problems that determines whether worry will rule our day. And like me, you are probably tired of worry being in charge.

## Worry-Free Exercise

**BODY:**

Review your family history and biology. Do you come from a line of worriers? If so, remember you are not a victim but must be more intentional in letting go of worry if you possess a predisposition toward it.

**SOUL:**

Think about the times you have experienced loss, trauma, or difficult experiences.

1. How did you respond to those circumstances?

2. Could any of these times have created a root of worry in your life?

3. Do you have unresolved grief related to losses in your life? Are you stuck in the grief process—still angry, depressed, shocked, trying to bargain with God—or have you moved through the emotions of grief and let go of the loss? Have you faced the pain?

**SPIRIT:**

What are your thoughts about God's involvement in the trauma or difficulty? Do you blame God, think He does not care about you, or believe He somehow does not love you?

Pray about any situation that has led to worry prompted by feelings of vulnerability, powerlessness, or lack of control. Ask God to reveal distrust, unbelief, or unresolved feelings. Submit those to God and ask Him to heal those hurts and speak His truth in to the situation. Then grieve the loss so you can move on and allow healing to progress.

Meditate on Psalm 23:1-6:

> *The LORD is my shepherd, I shall not be in want. He makes me lie down in green pastures, he leads me beside quiet waters, he restores my soul. He guides me in paths of righteousness for his name's sake.* Even though I walk through the valley of the shadow of death, I will fear no evil, for you are with me; your rod and your staff, they comfort me. *You prepare a table before me in the presence of my enemies. You anoint my head with oil; my cup overflows. Surely goodness and love will follow me all the days of my life, and I will dwell in the house of the LORD forever.*

Chapter 3

# Confessions of Worriers: Why We Do It

*People get so in the habit of worry that if you save*
*them from drowning and put them on a bank*
*to dry in the sun with hot chocolate and muffins*
*they wonder whether they are catching cold.*

**—JOHN JAY CHAPMAN**

There is an old saying in mental health. We do what we do because it is comfortable and familiar, and because it works for us in some strange way. In other words, we hang on to bad habits because they are old friends and help us for the moment. The habit may not be good for us or have a positive outcome, but it usually serves some kind of purpose.

With worry, the purpose it serves is what usually sustains it. Worriers believe they get something from worrying. Holding a positive belief about worry keeps worry going, even though the result is typically anxiety. To the worrier, worry works…despite the anxiety that comes along with it.

Worry is hard to give up when it is viewed as helpful. For example, if you believe worry can stop bad things from happening, then worrying is doing something useful. This positive belief about worry kicks in whenever bad things might happen.

In reality, worry does not stop bad things from happening. But since most of our worries never materialize, it seems like worry is doing the job.

## WHAT DO YOU BELIEVE ABOUT WORRY?

As you begin to consider what you believe worry does for you, ask yourself these five questions:

1. Do I think worry allows me to control external events?

2. Does worry make me productive or nonproductive?

3. Does worry make things seem important?

4. Do I worry as a way to show people I care?

5. Does worry prevent me from taking action because it feels like I am doing something?

In this chapter, the confessions of worriers will give us clues as to why people find it tough to let go of worry.

### Worry helps you prepare for the worst outcomes

Kristin loves her son, Mark, and does everything in her power to make sure he is successful in school. When he was called to the office for fighting, Kristin and her husband were rightfully upset. Even though fighting was prohibited, Kristin's husband felt their son had to defend himself against bullying to win the respect of his peers. Kristin was not so sure.

Worried that her son's aggression could escalate, Kristin began to rehearse all the bad things that could happen if her son was in a fight again. The more she obsessed on the possibility of his expulsion, the more real it became. Worry got the best of her. So much so that she made an appointment with a therapist to get help with her runaway thoughts.

As the therapist talked with Kristin, one thing became obvious. In her mind, worry worked. If she could imagine every possible negative thing that could happen, she felt prepared for a negative outcome. She hung on to worry because it helped her anticipate the future and be ready for bad news.

Kristin clung to worry because it was pretend control. Like Kristin, we may think that if we can imagine the worst-case scenario about a situation, we are prepared for bad news. This feels like control, but it is not.

To make matters worse, a great deal of time and energy is wasted anticipating what could happen in the future. But odds are that what you anticipate will not come true. According to a study in *Clinical Psychology and Psychotherapy*, 85 percent of the time people's worries never materialize.[1] (That fact alone can reinforce the idea that worrying somehow prevents negative outcomes.) But worrying does not make you more prepared for the future. It actually interferes with your ability to problem-solve. So does worry work to prepare you for future events? Not really.

**Worry helps you avoid negative and unpleasant outcomes**

Barry knew his job was on the line. After months of reporting late to work and lagging behind on productivity, the warnings from his boss were becoming more frequent. Manufacturing was down, and the company was going to make cuts. The thought of losing his job consumed Barry.

Every day he would talk to his co-workers about how the company was picking on him and that he would be the first to go during layoffs. His anxiety became so great that it made his productivity even worse. Since he was convinced he was the next person to be laid off, worry helped him avoid thinking about his bad work habits and the fact he would have to look for another job. Worry seemed to help calm his physical body and keep him from thinking about the reality of the layoff.

For Barry, worry served a purpose. Even though we know worry creates anxiety and stress on the body, excessive worry can actually reduce physical signs of agitation. It works like this. Worry involves negative thoughts. In excess, those worried thoughts fend off a high level of anxiety because they keep Barry from picturing the negative (telling his wife and family he lost his job). So as he obsessively worries about his job and allows that worry to make things worse in his daily performance, the worry prevents him from picturing the reality of what will likely happen. Worry actually distracts him from the upsetting picture of walking out of the company jobless.

When worry is used to keep frightening images away, it serves to manage fear in the short term. But it actually makes things worse over time. All of Barry's energy is directed toward worry and not toward the reality of a pending layoff and the need to find a new job.

People like Barry who use worry to avoid negative outcomes are likely to develop a generalized anxiety disorder. Worry is a way to stay distracted from highly emotional issues, and it becomes a coping style—one that eventually allows so much anxiety that it spreads to most areas of a person's life.

### Worry brings attention to important issues

Irene has several grandchildren. She prays for them to make good decisions. One of her granddaughters is dating a young man the family does not particularly like. Irene is very worried that her granddaughter will marry this man and have a terrible life. She has talked to her granddaughter about her concerns but still spends her days worrying about the relationship. She calls her son regularly to check on his daughter's status with this young man. She is not sleeping at night. Every conversation she has with her granddaughter focuses on the possible negative outcomes of this man remaining in her life.

The granddaughter is frustrated, does not appreciate the constant negative feedback, and wants Grandma to back off. She has tried several times to tell Grandma that worrying about this relationship is not helping it any. In fact, there is a part of her that wants to continue to date this guy just to prove Grandma wrong. Irene's response is telling: "I worry about you because you are important to me. You should worry if I don't worry!"

What Irene is saying here is that worry brings attention to an important issue. The person her granddaughter marries is important. In Grandma's way of thinking, if she did not worry, it would be a sign of not caring or minimizing the importance of this relationship in her granddaughter's life. Worry serves a function. It says, this issue is important, and I will show you how important it is by worrying about it.

### Worry is an attempt to problem-solve things that could happen

Libby's elderly parents have multiple health issues that make it difficult to stay in their home of 35 years. But they prefer to stay in their house no matter how challenging it is. It seems like every day a new challenge comes—Dad falls and hurts his leg; Mom feels dizzy from her diabetes and has to be checked regularly for insulin management; both are having problems getting up the stairs to their front door; Dad cannot run the lawn mower without stopping several times and resting; guardrails are needed on the bathtub so they can pull themselves up. The list goes on and on.

Libby does her best to keep up with these daily challenges and demands, but she is racked with worry. What if one of them falls and cannot get up? What if Mom's blood sugar becomes dangerously low and Dad is outside tending to the lawn? What if they slip on the stairs and hurt themselves? What if they miss the guardrail and slip and fall? The list of what-ifs has taken over Libby's mind. Her days are spent trying to anticipate every possible scenario that could befall her parents. If she can anticipate every problem, she can solve it and prevent bad things from happening. And while problem-solving is usually an antidote to worry, trying to solve problems that have not occurred instead brings on worry. It is also exhausting.

In Libby's mind, she can never do enough to bring problems to a satisfactory end. There is always one more scenario or potential danger she must anticipate in the hope of keeping her parents from disaster. She is racked with guilt over the idea that they could get hurt or be vulnerable. Thus, worrying seems like it is helping her problem-solve… but the problems have not happened and are based in what-if scenarios. Because Libby cannot anticipate every possible danger, her problem-solving never ends, and it brings on more worry.

Furthermore, even if worrying might be an attempt to problem-solve, it does not necessarily lead to action. A person can come up with all possible negative outcomes of a course of action but still not move forward with solutions. And some problems simply cannot be fixed.

## Worry motivates

It is time for midterm exams, and Jana has a borderline C in her chemistry class. She has to have a C to pass the course and is very worried because the midterm grade could make or break her final grade. As she studies, thoughts of failure continually pop into her head. Her mind is distracted from the material she needs to master by thoughts of failing and dropping out of college.

She calls a friend to study with her and explains how important this exam is to her. But she continues to obsess on worried thoughts. *What if I fail? How can I make up enough other work to bring the grade up? My parents will be so mad at me. How could I have let my grades slide to this point?* Worry after worry is spoken or thought.

Her friend tells her to stop. How is this helping her study? After Jana takes a deep breath and actually thinks about it, she realizes that in some weird way she believes worrying about the exam is motivating her to do well. The more she focuses on the need for a good grade, the more motivated she feels. However, the worry is blocking her ability to master the information. While it may feel like worry is motivating her, it is actually interfering with her ability to learn.

## Worry feels like we are doing something

Tony and Rhonda are struggling in their marriage. For a number of years, Tony has been addicted to pornography. Rhonda is a worried wreck. What if their children find out? What if their friends knew or, worse, their pastor? She is consumed with fear of the secret being found out, and she feels that worrying about her husband's problem is doing something.

It is not. Tony's problem needs to be addressed head-on, not worried over. The best thing would be to confront Tony and involve people in helping him. Rhonda feels that worrying about the consequences of the pornography problem is proactive. She is in denial. Worrying is doing nothing to help. In fact, the lack of confrontation makes it easier for Tony to continue.

She begins to obsess on things that are not the root of her husband's problem. Maybe if she loses weight and tries to act more interested in sex, her husband will stop looking at pornography. Maybe she has not been a good enough wife. Constant thoughts about what she should do swirl in her head. Worry, she admits, at least feels like she is doing something in a situation that feels very much out of her control. But is she? Not at all.

Tony has a serious addiction problem. Rhonda's worry with no steps of action will not change things. Tony needs to be confronted. He must own his problem and begin dealing with its fallout in the relationship. Rhonda's worrying is actually delaying necessary confrontation.

## Worry might affect the outcome

Sal was in an unhappy marriage. During the past few years, he and his wife had grown apart emotionally. They had allowed their busy lives to eat up any time to be together. Slowly, they drifted apart and allowed negative thoughts of each other build in the relationship. The process began with a little criticism, then more. That criticism led to feeling disappointed and hurt, and eventually feelings of discontent grew stronger. The more each felt the other was not meeting his or her need, the more defensive each became. Eventually, they stopped talking and became emotionally distant.

Sal saw what was happening. Instead of going to counseling or trying to talk to his wife, he worried. Would his wife be attracted to another man? Who was she confiding in these days? What was she talking about to other people? Did his wife still love him? How could he rescue this dying relationship? These worries built up as the relationship became more distant.

Left to his own thinking (because he was not talking to his wife), he built up a worry bank. Maybe all his worry would positively influence his marriage. If he worried about his wife, wasn't that a sign of caring? Wouldn't worry somehow make a difference, show her he cared? Unfortunately for Sal, *no*! Worry did not translate into action to improve the marriage. Worry did not solve the intimacy problems or tackle the issues that led to emotional distance. Worry did nothing but keep the couple stuck.

Do not think that worry does anything to change the outcome of difficult situations. It has no bearing on what happens. It only keeps you stuck and anxious.

## Worry does not do what we think it does

Based on these confessions, I hope you see that worry does not provide us with positive outcome or benefit. When we believe worry prepares us for the worst possible outcome, it does not. If we believe worry helps us avoid negative and unpleasant outcomes, it might for the moment, but not in the long run. We still have to face the issue involved in our worry.

We might think worry brings attention to important issues. It does, but negative attention causes mental, physical, and spiritual problems. It is much better to give positive attention to concerns. Also, we are kidding ourselves when we believe worry is a way to problem-solve. Nothing gets solved. And when we feel worry motivates or causes us to do something productive, we need to rethink this notion. Worry gets in the way of productivity.

So in order to say goodbye to worry, we have to give up the belief that worry helps us in the long run. The positive benefits we think we gain from worry do not exist. Bottom line, there is no good reason to worry.

## Worry-Free Exercise

### BODY:

As you read through this chapter, did you feel tense or anxious? If so, close your eyes, quiet your mind, and evaluate any stress that may have formed from thinking about worry. Visualize yourself in a calm place like a beach, sitting in front of a fireplace on a snowy night, or resting in the beauty of nature. Check your body again. Are you less tense? Picturing a quiet, restful scene can calm your physical body.

### SOUL:

Now that you have read this chapter, evaluate worry as a benefit in your life using the questions introduced earlier:

1. Do I think worry allows me to control external events?

2. Does worry make me productive or nonproductive?

3. Does worry make things seem important?

4. Do I worry as a way to show people I care?

5. Does worry prevent me from taking action because it feels like I am doing something?

If you answer *yes* to any of these questions, rethink the use of worry in your life. Have you allowed worry to serve a purpose that does not work? If so, are you willing to give up that belief in order to say goodbye to worry?

## SPIRIT:

Ask God to empower you through His Spirit to not use worry as a coping strategy. Meditate on 2 Corinthians 12:9:

> *He said to me, "My grace is sufficient for you, for my power is made perfect in weakness." There-fore I will boast all the more gladly about my weak-nesses, so that Christ's power may rest on me.*

Chapter 4

# Worried Sick:
# The Physical Toll of Worry

*Heavy thoughts bring on physical maladies;*
*when the soul is oppressed so is the body.*
—MARTIN LUTHER

W*orrywart* is a label given to someone who worries constantly about everything. You may have used the term to describe someone you know—or yourself. Though the origin of this term is not clear, the Oxford English Dictionary first used it to describe a neurotic group of residents in a mental hospital. That should tell us something!

Later, the word was used in popular culture by cartoonist James R. Williams in his 1922 to 1957 comic strip, "Out Our Way." The character who was considered to be a worrywart was not the one who worried. He, the worrywart, caused worry in others.

Today we joke about worrywarts and do not take them seriously. But we should. The truth is, worry does damage to body, soul, and spirit. Holistically, worry is wearisome. It depletes the body, discourages the soul, and dampens the spirit. Overall, worrying interferes with the joy of everyday living. No one wants to be a worrywart.

In this chapter, we will look at the impact of worry on the physical body and how a lack of self-care can trigger worry. Because worry affects our physical health, it is time to re-evaluate the way we live and make changes if needed.

## Women worry more than men

It turns out that worrywarts are more often women than men.[1] Some of you may think this is no surprise, but the reason for this difference is complex. It involves the way men and women think, feel, behave, and develop biologically. There is no one reason for it; rather, a number of factors form the greater sensitivity women seem to exhibit toward worry.

In our culture, worry is often viewed as a feminine trait and seen as a behavior associated with being female.[2] Not only is it more acceptable in our society for women to worry, but women also tend to internalize their problems, making it easier for them to worry.[3] And since worry is a type of internal coping, it makes sense that women worry more. We use worry as a coping skill.

However, the playing field is more equal when we consider *what* people worry about. Women and men have equal levels of worry about finances, the future, interpersonal relationships, and competence at work. For women, self-confidence plays a key role.[4] Thoughts such as, "Will I look stupid?" "Will he or she approve of me?" "Will I be able to handle this?" relate to a lack of confidence and can elevate feelings of failure and powerlessness over one's life. And because women often have lower status in the workplace and at home, the lack of confidence contributes to more stress that leads to worry.[5] Thus lack of self-confidence, more common in women than men, creates worry.

In a study published in the *Journal of Anxiety Disorders*, researchers concluded that women win the worry game because they engage more in what is called *thought suppression* (avoiding thoughts).[6] Thought suppression will be discussed in a later chapter because it is often used to try and stop worry. It does not work—but women still use it. Here is how it works.

Because the content of worry is usually negative (for example, my child could die, I could crash my car, and so on), women try to suppress the thoughts. But attempts to suppress a thought usually result in preoccupation with that thought (worry). The more you try *not* to think about a worry, the more you do. So telling yourself to stop worrying usually does not work.

In contrast to men, women tend to obsess more about their thoughts and think more about feelings. Men avoid worry thoughts and use distraction to cope. Distraction focuses thinking away from a specific worry.

Men do win the worry game when they believe that worry works for them in some useful way, as we discussed in the last chapter. So, when men believe worry helps them or is beneficial, they worry more than women. What you think about worry matters. (All of chapter 6 is devoted to the issue of worried thoughts.)

Finally, worry may be related to hormones. There is a biological difference that may impact the way men and women deal with stress interpersonally. Author Holly Stevens contends that the hormone difference between men and women plays a role in why women are better worriers. In her book *Women Who Worry Too Much*, she says that female hormones dampen the "fight-or-flight" response that occurs with stress. Instead of fighting or fleeing stress, women use a "tend-and-befriend" strategy. When they perceive danger or stress, their instincts are to take care of others (tend) and turn to social networks of supportive women (befriend). This tend-and-befriend coping style results in women avoiding threats more than men, and thus it reinforces anxiety and worry.[7]

## Worried sick

As mentioned, anxiety is a normal reaction to stress. When your body perceives a threat or danger, it tries to flee from that danger or stay and fight—the fight-or-flight mechanism mentioned above. During worry, the body behaves like it does when a threat is perceived. The body believes danger is present even though it is not. The brain triggers the fight-or-flight response in order to protect you. Your brain then remembers that trigger for the future, and anxiety is born. Chronic anxiety damages the body.

If you hold on to anxiety once the perceived threat or danger is over, you move from normal anxiety to worry. Worry keeps the mind in overdrive, and the physiological reaction of fight-or-flight (the surge of adrenaline that puts our bodies on alert) remains. The sympathetic nervous system continues to release stress hormones such as cortisol. These increased hormones raise blood-sugar levels and triglycerides, which can result in headaches, irritability, muscle aches and tensions, dizziness, difficulty swallowing, shortness of breath, dry mouth, fatigue, inability to concentrate, nausea, nervous energy, sweating, trembling, twitching, and others.[8] And when stress triggers excessive worry, a chronic state of anxiety leads to immune suppression, digestive problems, muscle tension, short-term memory loss, premature coronary artery disease, and even heart attack.

Ken's doctor believed a state of worry was the source of his heart problems. After going over multiple stresses in his life, the doctor asked Ken, "So what do you do to release all that stress?" Ken could not come up with an answer. The more he thought about it, the more he realized he mostly worried and had no outlet to reduce stress. He had never considered that worry could be placing him in physical danger.

Rachel had a similar experience with her doctor. After several rounds of sickness, her doctor felt that her constant worry was suppressing her immune system, making her more susceptible to illness. Until she learned how to let go of negative thoughts and relax more, illness would be a part of her life.

### Worry is bad for your heart

Worry impacts every system in the body. It raises blood pressure and cholesterol, increases blood clotting, and creates headaches; back pain; stomachaches, and more.[9] As Ken found out, the heart is no exception. Worry activates the cardiovascular system in a negative way. Here is why.

When we worry, we keep stress at the forefront of our thinking. Worry creates a cognitive representation (a thought) about stress that keeps this negativity going in our minds. Continuing to think about the negative thought through worry arouses our bodies.[10] The result of this arousal is an elevated heart rate.

Worry is also a form of self-talk. It is made up of thoughts and is an internal monologue. It works to avoid feared events this way. When you *visualize* an image of something feared, the impact on your body is stronger than if you simply *think* about the feared event. Specifically, researchers found that mentally picturing a feared event elicits a stronger cardiovascular response than thinking about that event.[11] Thus, your body gets less physically aroused when you think worried thoughts than if you picture the feared event. In essence, worried thoughts calm the body more than visualizing problems. Worry lowers physical arousal because it involves thoughts not images.

### Job worries especially stress the heart

Researchers in the Netherlands and at Ohio State University found that the strongest effects on the heart came from worry involving work-related stress and worry about future issues.[12] In terms of job stress, it was the moment-to-moment worries on the job that were the source of concern. When our worries are specific to work, the impact to the heart is shown to be as great as smoking (a risk factor for cardiovascular disease). And anticipatory stress (worrying about things that have not yet occurred) causes cardiac activation regardless of whether or not the stress ever pans out.

A group of researchers associated with a study at the Harvard School of Public Health also concluded that high levels of worry increase coronary heart disease.[13] Since worry is part of anxiety and anxiety is related to increased incidence of coronary heart disease, it makes sense that it would increase the risk for this disease. The point is that worry does more than produce an anxious feeling; it wreaks havoc on the heart and the rest of the body.

### Five changes to eliminate the negative

Not only does worry put you at risk for cardiovascular problems, it can actually lead to unhealthy habits that make you likely to die younger than a non-worrier. Researchers at Purdue University found that men who are natural-born worriers drink, smoke, and develop other unhealthy habits to deal with their worry. These habits raise mortality rates.[14] So if you are prone to worry, evaluate your lifestyle. You may need to make a few adjustments in order to reduce your tendency toward anxiety and worry. Here are a number of suggestions.

### Eating habits

Begin with your eating habits. Sugary snacks and high amounts of refined sugar can cause blood sugar to rise and then fall sharply, leaving you feeling emotionally and physically drained. So eliminate as much refined sugar from your diet as possible. This means saying no to sodas, fruit drinks, and coffees and teas loaded with sugar, eating fewer desserts, and monitoring portion size when you do indulge.

Simple starches are also quickly converted to sugar in the body, so reducing or eliminating pastas, refined cereals, chips, and white bread and eating more whole grains, vegetables, and other complex carbohydrates helps. Do not skip breakfast or other meals. Eat small meals during the day. When you go too long without eating, blood sugar falls and you can feel anxious and irritable.

Excessive use of salt also stresses the body. It can deplete potassium, a mineral you need for proper functioning of your nervous system, and it also raises blood pressure. Raised blood pressure puts extra strain on your heart and arteries. Sodium (salt) is in a number of processed foods. Look for foods that are labeled low sodium or salt free. And go easy on that saltshaker sitting on your kitchen table.

### Using caffeine

Caffeine can increase anxiety, interfere with your sleep, and even trigger panic attacks in some people. It is a stimulant that aggravates anxiety. When I was in college, I used to drink black coffee every night in order to stay awake to study. Some nights I would down as many as ten cups. The coffee kept me alert and awake, but it also put my body in a state of stress. I began to notice that I had overall feelings of anxiety and worry. This was directly related to the amount of caffeine I was ingesting. I stopped drinking coffee and my symptoms of anxiety disappeared. Too much caffeine can make a person tense and vulnerable to increased anxiety.

Caffeine is found not only in coffee and teas but also in sodas and a number of medications. Be sure to check the packaging to know if you are getting a dose of caffeine. And if you are sensitive to caffeine, lower your daily dose.

### Sleepless in Seattle and every other city in America

It will come as no surprise that according to researcher Thomas Borkovec at Penn State University, worry plays a role in insomnia.[15] Borkovec and his colleagues found that intrusive thoughts create sleeplessness.

When you chronically worry, it does not matter how sleepy you are. The worried thoughts marching around in your head keep you on active alert.

Jennifer knows this all too well. A single mother with an autistic son and an active daughter, Jennifer's day is beyond busy. Her mental activity is in overdrive: How will she will pay her bills, find services for her child, deal with day care, and be productive on her job? At night, she is unable to shut off the thoughts of the day and tosses and turns most of the night, rehearsing ways to bring in more money and cover her family's needs.

Because of Jennifer's constant worry, her adrenaline stays high, causing her sympathetic nervous system to go into overdrive. Dr. Donna Arand of Kettering Hospital's Sleep Disorders Center in Dayton, Ohio, describes what is happening to Jennifer this way—she is running in fifth gear instead of second. Given Jennifer's genetics, childhood experiences, her poor diet, lack of exercise and support, and the number of stressors she experiences every day, it is no wonder she cannot sleep at night. Her mind does not turn off the concerns of the day. She has developed a pattern of chronic insomnia. And according to Dr. Arand, even when stress is eliminated, insomnia can continue because it has become a pattern.[16]

Worry must be turned off. Sometimes it helps to keep a pad of paper near your bed and simply write down the things that concern you at night. This strategy puts the concerns on paper and helps you remember to address them in days to come.

Another way to help clear your mind is to develop what doctors call good sleep hygiene. Sleep hygiene is a series of steps you can take to assist you in falling asleep. Sometimes the lack of getting rest has to do with the way we approach sleep. Sleep hygiene recommendations include the following:

1. Avoid or limit caffeine, nicotine, and alcohol at night.
2. Drink enough water to keep you from being thirsty but not so much that you get up during the night.
3. Check all your medications to see if there is a side effect related to sleep.

4. Make exercise a regular part of your life, but do not do it late at night.

5. Avoid eating heavy meals at night.

6. Relax before bed with a quiet activity. Maybe read a book, listen to soothing music, soak in a bathtub, and so on.

7. Arrange your bedroom to be quiet, dark, and cool. Bright light and stimulating colors can keep you alert.

8. Use your bed for only sleep and sexual intimacy.

9. Purchase a comfortable mattress and pillow.

10. Develop a routine of waking and going to sleep at the same time every day and night. It is best not to nap during the day. And if you cannot sleep, get up and do something rather than tossing and turning for hours.[17]

Good sleep hygiene sets the stage for a good night's rest.

### Smoking

Have you ever said, "I smoke because it calms me down. I need cigarettes to relax me"? You may be surprised to learn that this is *not* true. Smoking does not calm you or relieve stress. In fact, smokers have higher rates of stress than nonsmokers. Why? Nicotine dependency actually exacerbates stress. Yet most smokers surveyed believe smoking relaxes them.

Since we know that nicotine does not calm people (it is not a sedative), why are smokers more irritable and feel they need to smoke to relax? It is the *lack* of nicotine between smokes that causes a regular smoker to be irritable and stressed. In other words, irritability and stress build up during periods when you do *not* smoke. Smoking reverses the tension and irritability that comes from nicotine abstinence. As you withdraw from nicotine between smokes, you feel irritable. Smoking stops that temporary withdrawal.

In a study by researchers Parrott and Garnham,[18] smoker stress was found to be the same as nonsmokers. During periods of nicotine abstinence, however, smokers actually had worse stress levels. So instead of reducing anxiety, smoking caused more.

Now you're saying, "Okay—but when I quit, I am more stressed." Again, not so. According to research, quitting reduces stress. No studies found former smokers more stressed than those who continued to smoke. What researchers did observe was that in the first few days after quitting, people have more anger, anxiety, and restlessness. Two weeks later, people settle down and eventually report improved mood.[19]

So the next time you think, "Smoking relaxes me," you are misinformed. Not only is nicotine highly addictive, but it can create stress as well. Hopefully, this will give you another good reason to stop smoking. And if someone tries to tell you he or she cannot quit because of stress, help them understand that quitting is exactly what he or she needs to do to *reduce* stress.

### Alcohol

The use of alcohol can also bring on worry. Even though a small amount relaxes you for the moment, the long-term effects of using drinking to cope are serious. Drinking to curb anxiety or worry can lead to alcohol abuse and even dependence. And if the reason you drink is because you feel insecure or inadequate, alcohol may make those feelings even worse because people do things under the influence they would not normally do.

Also, while small amounts of alcohol may relax you, high amounts promote anxiety and interfere with sleep. Bottom line: Alcohol is not a treatment for worry. Consuming too much can lead to an irregular heartbeat and lowered blood sugar, both of which can bring on increased symptoms of anxiety. Using alcohol as a relaxation method carries the risk of dependence and abuse.

### Three changes to add the positive

### Exercise

Exercise is a natural stress-reliever. You may know how important exercise is but still do not do it! Yet its benefits are enormous. It can reduce muscle tension and frustration and naturally relaxes the body. So why don't we regularly exercise? Either we do not have a moment to fit it in our day or we do not enjoy it. For some of you, both reasons may be true.

The solution is to make time and choose exercises you enjoy. In terms of time, you probably think it is impossible to commit to exercise. So the best strategy is to think about exercise like taking your vitamins. Don't think too much about it, just do it! Do not make excuses or talk yourself out of doing it. Make exercise a scheduled activity that is nonnegotiable. Fit it in somewhere. We make time for things that are important to us.

In terms of how you exercise, it is important to choose something you enjoy or at least can tolerate. For example, I tried running. I gave it six months, did it six days a week, and hated it. I am not a runner, but put me on a pair of Rollerblades and I can have a good time. For me, rollerblading or playing tennis is enjoyable—running is not. If running is my activity, the likelihood of my exercising is low. I will find an excuse not to do it.

Experiment with different types of exercise to find activities you like. There are so many options: bike riding, dancing, skating, basketball, tennis, skiing, walking, table tennis—anything that gets you active and off that couch. Try to do at least 30 minutes of exercise every day. It will boost your energy and activate brain chemicals that make you feel good. It does not have to be drudgery. And even if it feels like drudgery, you will notice an improvement in worry. Sometimes we do things we do not like just because we are grown-ups!

### Find ways to relax

We all need downtime. Therefore, identify ways to relax and rejuvenate your body and mind. Relaxation is not something you do once a year on a cruise to the Bahamas (although this can't hurt). Relaxing should be a regularly practiced part of your life. You need balance in all things. Even God rested on the seventh day of creation! Relaxation prevents stress from building up and provides an avenue for releasing tension.

Take a moment and think about how you relax. Is it with TV and a shot of alcohol? Or do you mindlessly eat while sitting in front of your computer? Whatever you do, try to think of ways to relax that are healthy and calm the body, soul, and spirit. Ideas include a meditative walk, a hot bath, reading a portion of Scripture, resting on a beach, listening to relaxing music, playing golf.

### DO YOU USE TIME WISELY?

Poor time management can be another source of lifestyle stress. You have only so much time in a day, so it is important to learn to prioritize and be realistic about goals. If you are a person who spends energy on things that are unproductive or take too much time, you may need to learn better time management. Time management maximizes your efforts. There are books and websites dedicated to learning it, but here are a few tips to get you started.

Plan your day. A "things-to-do list" helps organize and prioritize activities. Write down what you need to accomplish for the day. Then prioritize the list so you do not spend time on activities that are not that important for the day. And for those of you who tend to put things off and then find yourself rushing at the last minute, a list can prevent procrastination.

### *Be assertive and set boundaries*

Learn to say *no* to things that distract you and take too much of your time. If you find yourself saying things like, "Sure, I'll cook for the spaghetti dinner"; "Yes, I can babysit your children for the day"; "Yes, I can chair another committee"; "Since no one else will volunteer, I guess I'll do it," you may be overcommitting. As a result, you become stressed and kick yourself for not saying no.

Too many of us take on too much and fail to set healthy boundaries because we do not use the word *no*. We are afraid to speak up, do not feel we have the right, need to please others, want to be loved for what we do, or think we have to be superhuman and do it all! Time to turn in your cape! Learn to say no and not feel guilty. You will reduce stress in your life.

Saying no requires assertiveness. Assertiveness is behavior that falls somewhere in the middle between giving in and aggressiveness. It is not giving in to the wants of others or keeping silent and expecting people to read your mind. It is also not yelling at people and demanding your way. It is a practiced skill that helps you manage stress. Contrary to popular thought, you do not have to be angry to be assertive. In fact, I prefer you stay calm.

There are two parts involved in being assertive: 1) know what you want; 2) say it. One of the reasons people are not assertive is because they do not know what they want. They are wishy-washy, unsure, and undefined in what they think or feel. They allow others to manipulate them into doing things and then feel resentful because they have too much to do. Or they feel guilty and do not believe they have the right to speak up. They ask, "Who am I to say no?" You are someone important. You are also responsible for managing stress that comes your way. When you can do something about stress, take the initiative—speak up! Know what you want and take a reasonable position. Do not feel guilty setting limits. Reduce stress by taking control where and when you can.

If you do not speak up and let your voice be heard, anger and resentment will grow. Oftentimes, these are roots of depression, anxiety, and eating disorders. Many of my female patients have to be taught how to be assertive because it is a skill they never learned. It is also something that has to be practiced. The benefits from speaking up are improved physical and psychological health. Your relationships will improve and you will better manage stress. In addition, you will gain respect from people. They may not like your stand, but they will respect you for taking one.

**Worry and emotional well-being**

Not only does our physical health suffer when worry turns to anxiety, but our emotional well-being is affected too. When worry takes over and becomes what is called a generalized anxiety disorder (GAD), it makes life difficult. People with GAD know they are excessive worriers but have difficulty stopping worried thoughts. Worry becomes an illness, an illness that is mental in origin but impacts the physical body.

John was recently diagnosed with GAD. His life was unmanageable because worry intruded on his ability to do his job. As an architect, he worried about making a mistake on his drawings, miscalculating numbers, forgetting important information, losing jobs for the company, being laid off, losing promotions to younger men, pleasing his bosses, and carrying enough of the load for the entire team. These types of thoughts flooded his thinking to the point that he could hardly complete his drawings and was late turning in projects. He spent his off hours worrying about his ability to perform at work. He could not relax at home, was irritable with the kids, and found himself turning to alcohol to relax his body and thoughts.

John's family noticed how worry impacted all areas of his life and decided to call a mental-health counselor for an evaluation. During the interview, John admitted feeling out of control but not able to stop obsessing on that feeling. He was not sleeping at night and his marriage was falling apart because he could not relax enough to be with his family and enjoy life. His wife described living with him as constantly being on edge. His level of anxiety was taking a toll on everyone.

John's story is typical of the symptoms associated with GAD. They include restlessness or feeling keyed up or on edge, fatigue, difficulty concentrating or having your mind go blank, irritability, muscle tension, and sleep disturbance. There may also be cold, clammy hands, dry mouth, sweating, nausea or diarrhea, urinary frequency, trouble swallowing, depression and exaggerated startle response. [20]

When a person suffers with GAD, anxiety disrupts work, social life, and family life. The amount of anxiety felt is excessive and chronic. Worry feels completely out of control, and professional help is usually needed. Treatment involves a type of therapy that looks at worried thoughts with the intent of challenging those thoughts and changing them. In addition, making lifestyle changes such those discussed above are recommended. Furthermore, learning and practicing relaxation techniques, knowing how to soothe yourself and quiet your mind, are all part of the treatment. If you need help, contact a mental-health professional.

### Medications to calm the body

I am often asked about the use of medications to relax the body. I usually recommend that people first try nonmedication strategies to lower anxiety. With changes in nutrition, exercise, and self-talk and a more relaxed approach to life, most people can move out of worry-wart status. However, depending on the level of anxiety and panic you experience, there are times when antianxiety medications can be useful.

In my own practice, I would recommend that people be evaluated for medication when they were so flooded with anxiety they could not work on making changes or concentrate on learning to cope differently. Medication often helped to accomplish the above. Once armed with new tools and coping skills, their medication was gradually discontinued. I say this because I do not want anyone who is using antianxiety medication appropriately to feel condemned.

Once a level of control is found that allows a person to work in therapy, the person can eventually discontinue the medication. This is especially true when treating panic attacks and phobias. This does not mean that medication must be used. It is simply a tool in the strategy box. Medications have proven to be effective for the treatment of obsessive-compulsive disorders (OCD). OCD is a psychiatric mental disorder classified as an anxiety disorder. It is characterized by unwanted thoughts and compulsive behavior that interfere with living. It involves a number of fears, such as fears of contamination, being harmed, making mistakes, or behaving in socially unacceptable ways; doubt, religious concerns, and sexual concerns. Compulsions can include hand washing, checking, collecting or hoarding, counting and repeating, and touching or tapping.

Specific areas of the OCD brain have been identified to be overactive, so there appears to be an organic basis. Current thought is that OCD is predisposed genetically and dormant until major stress activates it. Best practice is that medication be used in conjunction with cognitive behavioral therapy. Medication is not a cure for OCD and its long-term effectiveness is not always consistent.

The use of medication for any anxiety issue is usually a personal decision related to your values. There is much to consider when taking a medication. Medications provide symptom relief but do not get at the root cause of a disorder. And they have side effects that must be weighed. Some people cannot tolerate the side effects or are not willing to take the associated risks. Medications can also be expensive. If you do decide to use a medication, you should always be under the care of a physician and be regularly evaluated. I strongly recommend evaluation by a psychiatrist to discuss antianxiety medications if you choose to go that route. Psychiatrists are medical doctors trained in the use of these medications. They are familiar with side effects and dosing.

### How to relax your body

When I was in full-time private practice, I had a couch in my office. I used it mainly to help people learn to relax their bodies. Over the years, I noticed that people who grew up in the homes of an addict, alcoholic, abuser, or mentally unstable person carried a great deal of tension in their bodies even when that stress was no longer present. Growing up in an unpredictable household often led to a chronic state of physical tension. Most adults who came for therapy knew this tension as a normal state of being. So the idea that they were tense and could relax was often a foreign thought.

To help a person learn to relax, I would have him or her lie down on my couch with a soft blanket over his or her body. Then we would begin something called progressive muscle relaxation. This technique is based on the idea that muscles can be relaxed by tensing them for a few seconds, and then releasing the tension. For example, clench your right fist and hold the tension…now relax it. Do it again. Do the same with each muscle in your body. Progressively work through all your muscles and relax each of them. As you work through the various muscle groups by tensing and releasing, relaxation occurs. You can do this exercise any time of day or night. The more you practice tensing and relaxing your muscles, the easier it becomes. Then when you are aware of tension in your body, you can cue your body to relax. Practice makes this easy to do.

This type of relaxation can be used in everyday situations. In fact, I used this technique to overcome a bad experience at the dentist office. I used to be afraid of going to the dentist because, as a child, I had had a number of bad experiences. My cue to start feeling anxious was scheduling an appointment. By the time I arrived at the dentist and sat down in the chair, my body was very tense. I would think thoughts like, *What if it hurts? What if I need to have work done and get a shot? What if he misses and hits a nerve?* In order to change this, I practiced progressive muscle relaxation.

After several weeks of practice, I could cue my body to relax by telling myself "relax." Then when I sat in the dental chair, I did the relaxation. Once I knew I could relax my body and stay calm, worry was no longer a part of the time leading up to my visits. To this day, I do not look forward to going to the dentist, but I no longer worry ahead of time. And when I am in the chair and begin to feel tension in my body, I cue myself to relax and focus on doing so. A side benefit is that the more I relax, the less it hurts.

Progressive muscle relaxation is an especially effective technique for people who carry tension in their muscles. Tension and relaxation cannot coexist. Although I practiced progressive muscle relaxation with clients in my office, you can purchase a CD that will lead you through this exercise as well. Moreover, there are free downloads online that can be used to practice. The goal is to learn to relax the various muscle groups.

In therapy, clients are asked to practice progressive relaxation daily until they have a sense of how to relax their physical bodies. Then, whenever tension rises, they know how to cue their bodies to relax. This technique can be used while sitting in traffic, in a waiting room, at a work desk, and so on. The more you practice, the easier it will be to cue your body to relax when tension is noticed.

### Self-soothing

Another way to calm your physical body is to engage in activities that are self-soothing, which involves using the senses to calm down. Self-soothing activities lessen stress by providing positive stimulation. So, for example, lighting an aromatic candle, petting the dog, drinking a cup of warm tea, watching the sunset, and so on are positive ways to engage the senses. When stress hits hard, you can choose to do something in the moment that will calm you down. Self-soothing activities can relax you immediately and contribute to your well-being.

Here are a few more ideas. They are similar to relaxation activities:

- take a relaxing bath or hot shower
- organize something
- pray
- take a walk
- listen to soothing music
- clean
- go for a car ride
- phone a friend
- write a note to someone you care about
- watch a sunrise on the beach
- get a massage
- watch a funny movie
- play the piano or other musical instrument
- sit in a park and enjoy the beauty of nature
- visit a pet store
- try a new food recipe
- study a painting
- go for a swim

The idea is to exercise self-care when tension builds and engage in something soothing to the senses. Instead of shopping, drinking, gambling, numbing yourself with pain medication, or using some other unhealthy quick fix for stress, choose an activity that will calm you immediately and soothe your body and soul.

∽

In sum, chronic worry takes a toll on our physical and emotional health. Do not become a worrywart or allow worry to rule your life. Instead, learn to calm your physical body. A good night's sleep just might depend on it!

## Worry-Free Exercise

**BODY:**

Evaluate your lifestyle habits that may contribute to worry. What specifically could you change to help eliminate worry?

_____ Revise eating habits

_____ Reduce or eliminate caffeine

_____ Reduce or eliminate alcohol

_____ Stop smoking

_____ Create better sleep habits using sleep hygiene ideas

_____ Exercise regularly

_____ Incorporate relaxation into my life

_____ Practice relaxing my body using progressive muscle relaxation

_____ Engage in self-soothing activities

_____ Call a mental health professional if I think I may suffer from excessive anxiety

**SOUL:**

Learn no say NO to create more balance in your life.

Be assertive and set boundaries.

**SPIRIT:**

Meditate on Psalm 112:7-8:

> *He will have no fear of bad news; his heart is steadfast, trusting in the LORD. His heart is secure, he will have no fear; in the end he will look in triumph on his foes.*

And Matthew 11:28:

> *Come to me, all you who are weary and burdened, and I will give you rest.*

Chapter 5

# Worry Began in a Garden:
# The Spiritual Roots of Worry

*When worry is present, trust cannot crowd its way in.*
**—BILLY GRAHAM**

Worry is one of those irritating things in life we work hard to try to handle. But most of the time, we give little thought to its spiritual significance. Worry has a spiritual root that is usually ignored in our progressive culture. From a spiritual perspective, worry is challenging. At least it is for me! As mentioned in this book's introduction, it is not enough to manage worry. According to Scripture, we are instructed to eliminate it.

Saying goodbye to worry is not my idea. It is God's. Philippians 4:6 says, "Do not be anxious about anything..." Honestly, this is a tough Bible verse, one that seems almost impossible. And there are no qualifiers. I have looked for them. They do not exist. My natural reaction to this verse is, "Really, are You kidding, God? Maybe in ancient days but not today." Yet God's message does not change with the times. His Word is the same yesterday, today, and forever. God knows what our lives are like today. He did not say, "For those of you living in the twenty-first century, you can worry sometimes about some things. I totally understand." God unequivocally says, "Don't worry about anything." We all need God's grace to carry out this command.

### Worry's sordid origin

The setting was an exquisite garden occupied by one man, one woman, and creatures big and small. Clear blue skies and lots of sunshine gave way to beautiful, fragrant nights. No rain. The Creator walked and talked with the man and woman every day. From the moment He breathed life into the man, love existed. The Creator loved His creations and gave the man and woman just one instruction—eat whatever you like, but not the fruit of one specific tree.

Unbeknownst to the man and woman, a trap was set by one of the Creator's other creations. A garden creature, a snake, devised a plan to deceive the woman. He approached her with a tantalizing idea—eat fruit from the one prohibited tree and be like the Creator. The woman thought about this. She loved the Creator. Why would she not want to be like Him? The fruit, like the rest of creation, looked so appealing. So she ate and gave the fruit to her husband. He ate as well.

After eating, the couple knew they had sinned. Suddenly their eyes were opened to the reality of the disobedience. Guilt and shame flooded them. How would their Creator deal with their clear disobedience? What would He do? These were untested waters.

The couple hid from their Creator, fearing the outcome of their disobedience. When the Creator found them, just the sound of His voice caused fear in their hearts. Fear led to hiding and avoiding the One they loved.

Rather than hiding, they could have trusted their Creator and faced Him. After all, His love for them was demonstrated every day. Instead, they allowed shame and fear of the unknown to overwhelm that love. They were vulnerable and powerless against the Creator. Through sin, worry entered the world—a dreadful beginning.

Sin created a separation from the Creator. Once the couple chose the path of sin, they became like God in knowing the difference between good and evil. At that point, the Creator had no choice but to banish them from the garden. Out of love, He had to protect them from making an eternal mistake—because there was one other tree in the garden that was now a problem, the Tree of Life. If the couple was allowed to stay in the garden, they might also eat of that tree and live forever. The Creator's love for them refused to let this happen. Rather than allowing them to eat of the Tree of Life and live eternally in their sin and decaying state, Love chose the lesser of two evils. Drive them out of the garden and protect them from eternal suffering and decay. Suffering would be limited for a time. The Creator had a plan of redemption that would later be fulfilled by His Son.

Once the first couple left the beautiful garden, life changed. They were now physically separated from God. Without personal contact with Him, worry was set into motion. Pain and suffering entered the Earth. Today, we live in that fallen world and have not yet been removed from all suffering. Suffering, hardship, and alienation from God can produce worry.

## Job thwarts worry's momentum

As you can see, worry is a part of both ancient and modern times. Biblical Job is a prime example of how worry could have overtaken a life full of uncertainty. Job's life spun completely out of his control (through no fault of his own) when God decided to allow Satan to unleash unexplained suffering in his life.

Job, an upright and blameless man, was chosen by the Creator to be a part of a cosmic test. The challenge from Satan to God was this: If all that Job has is taken away, see if he still trusts You. If Job's life became full of calamity, the bet was that he would no longer trust God but give in to fear and worry.

God, the Creator, knew better. And while the end result of Job's testing was that he did indeed continue to trust in God and form a deeper intimacy with Him, Job endured immense suffering along the way. His struggles help us see how tempting it is to allow worry to take over.

When the cosmic test was in full force, Job lamented that the very thing he feared had come upon him. Chapter after chapter, he agonizes over the events unfolding in his life. He is baffled. Every loss and tragedy that befalls him is an opportunity to curse God and walk away from his life of faith. And the one closest to him who loved him, his wife, urged him to give in to worry and die. Who would blame him?

What makes Job's ultimate response amazing is that he had no idea what was happening behind the scenes. From his perspective, he was living a righteous life and loving God and then got blasted with bad things. His perspective on suffering was challenged. In his culture, good things were supposed to happen to good people, not bad things. His life of sudden suffering made no sense. No wonder he agonized and worked his way through worry.

### Undeserved suffering

Job helps us. His suffering was undeserved, a result of the prince of darkness being given reign on this earth for a limited time. God gave Satan permission to torment Job, a fact to which Job was not privy. The likelihood that Job would give up on God given the suffering that came his way is what Satan bet on. But God knew better. Job would not give up on Him just because everything in his life fell apart. He allowed the test in order to prove that Job loved Him no matter what happened. Would Job curse Him and die when suffering hit, or would Job trust and love Him despite his circumstances?

Job's response to undeserved suffering is one that speaks loudly to all of us. Will we lay aside our worry and trust God when things look difficult, when trauma and loss enter our lives, when genetics predispose us to worry? Or will we walk away from God and decide to go it alone?

How many of us wrongly believe that when we suffer, it is God's punishment because of our sin? The book of Job corrects this thinking. When Job's friends put forth this argument—sin is the cause of your misfortunes—Job knows in his heart this is not true. Even though he has no explanation for his sudden tragedies, he refuses to give in to such thinking and give up on God.

When his friends question his faith and accuse him of sin, Job's faith does waver. And this is where we see worry enter the picture. He anguishes before God and allows doubt. His wife tempts him to curse God and die. His friends misread him.

### Job's conclusions

Despite the evidence and temptation to give up on God, Job finally concludes that God loves him. But to make sense of it all, he also demands an explanation from God. Any thinking person would ask why suffering happens. I love that God allows Job's questioning. But I'm upset that God never tells Job about the behind-the-scenes drama that is playing out. To the reader of the book, it does not seem fair that Job is not given an explanation. To God, it makes perfect sense. Without an explanation, Job will have to decide if he still trusts God. Trust is an act of faith. It is believing God when the evidence does not support His goodness. Faith says He is good no matter what we see in the moment.

God responds to Job's anguish by telling him that he has a limited view of running the universe. Basically—Job, you are puny and I am not. And Job repents by telling God that all his worry and anguish were born out of what he did not understand. In that moment, he grasps the bigness of God and sees how limited his perspective really is.

God does not get mad at Job for lamenting, anguishing, and questioning. His concerns mattered to God. God understands the mind and soul He created. But He is clear with Job that he cannot know the grander plan for his life. And this is how Job helps us with worry. Whatever the situation, we must be careful not to doubt God, or think that He makes us suffer out of some ghoulish need to punish us, or give up on Him because we think He has abandoned us.

In his book *A Long Obedience in the Same Direction,* Eugene Peterson says, "Relax. We are secure. God is running the show. Neither our feelings of depression nor the facts of suffering nor the possibilities of defection are evidence that God has abandoned us."[1] He is with us in the pain.

God is ultimately in control of our lives. And while suffering and difficulty come, He wants us to trust His love for us. Faith is about what we do not see. Do we believe God is ultimately for us? If we do, we do not have to worry about tomorrow or even today. Because if He is for us, who could possibly win against us? He is in our day, He is in our tomorrow, and He has the bigger picture. But the ultimate test for us is whether or not we believe He works on our behalf no matter what we see in the natural.

After Job's suffering, there was a shift in his relationship with God.

The test of faith eventually brought him to a new intimacy. His knowledge of God was replaced with his experience of God. He understood how big the God he served was and how small and limited he was in comparison.

And when God personally met Job in the middle of his suffering, He caused Job's doubts to vanish. God's presence is what melts away fear and worry. And His presence is with us today. In the middle of circumstances, do we conclude what Job did—that God can be trusted?

### CRY OUT ABOUT YOUR WORRIES

The book of Psalms provides insight into the many emotions that come in living through difficulty with God by our side. A spiritual base for conquering worry is repeatedly given. We see that life with God does not prevent feelings of sadness, anger, anguish, loss, abandonment, and so on. Instead, the Psalms journal the moods and emotions of people as they cry out to God. Numerous concerns are listed. But the conclusion is what counts.

The cares of life do not become worry when we are confident that we can bring them to God. A strong and loving God can handle what we throw at Him. No matter what we face, whatever the emotional roller coaster associated with worrisome circumstances, the Psalms conclude that the mighty power of God always prevails. In our distress, we cry to God and He hears us (Psalm 120). If it were not for the Lord... where would we be (Psalm 124)?

The Psalms point us in the right direction: Direct your feelings to God. He can handle them. Don't worry. There is hope. Believe that you matter to Him, and do not get lost in the circumstances around you. No matter how bleak things look in the present, He can be trusted.

### Worry as sin

In the spiritual world, worry is an indication of doubt and distrust.

It usually leads to sin. Perhaps we do not want to think about worry as potent or even embrace the idea that worry can become sin. In our minds, to worry is not like breaking the Ten Commandments. Those are big sins. But in God's eyes, sin is sin. He does not divide sins into big and small ones, important or unimportant ones, and He certainly does not change what is sin from generation to generation. Only we try to do that.

Now, I realize that when we talk about worry leading to sin, it may upset some of you. It is convicting because we all worry, myself included. And that is why we need to understand worry and work to change the acceptance of it in our everyday lives. And with any struggle that involves living more like Christ, we accept His grace. His grace covers us as we work through releasing worry.

When worry does lead to sin, we must repent. In repentance, we confess and turn from worry and go another direction. And as we consecrate our lives to God, He does not leave us on our own to master worry. He is deeply involved in the process and helps us overcome it. For most of us, this will require a careful look at our beliefs and assumptions about God and life. It means examining our habits and thoughts and lining them up with a true picture of who God is and His involvement in our lives.

### Jesus takes on worry

In Matthew's Gospel, chapter 6, Jesus brings up the topic of worry. He used the Greek word *merimnao*, which comes from the root word *merizo*, meaning "to divide or separate into parts."[2] The root meaning relates to being distracted or preoccupied with things that create anxiety, to be troubled with cares.

Jesus spoke against such a condition in our hearts, reminding His followers that the heavenly Father is always mindful of our needs. Thus, there is no need to worry. The illusion of control we think we have is not there. As Bobby McFerrin cheerfully reminded us in the 1988 song "Don't Worry, Be Happy," this sentiment is not a denial of life's problems, but an acknowledgment of where our confidence ultimately lies—with God, not ourselves. And that is the reason we can be concerned about life, but not worry.

Jesus admonishes us not to worry because it does not add a single day to our lives. He reminds us that if the Father cares for the birds, He will care for us, the crowning glory of His creation. Worry is useless. It is only through radical trust in Him that we can conquer worry daily.

### Eyes fixed on God, not circumstances

Like the apostle Peter, if we keep our eyes fixed on Christ, we can walk through any storm and not be afraid. With the sea raging around him, Peter had to step out in faith to meet the Lord, who was miraculously walking on the water toward him. Bold Peter decided to meet the Lord on the water. The minute he took his eyes off the Lord and became afraid, he began to sink. For a moment, he underestimated Jesus' power, presence, and knowledge of his troubles. But to his credit, Peter shifted from doubt to what he knew to be true. As Jesus' disciple, Peter had enough experience to know that the Lord would not allow him to sink if he stayed focused on Him.

When Peter began to sink, Jesus said to him, "You of little faith… why did you doubt?" (Matthew 14:31). Jesus sees the momentary doubt and questions it. The question directs Peter to stop looking at the natural experience and look at God. This encounter taught him to trust the Lord.

The same is true for us today. When the storms of life swirl around us and we take our eyes off of Christ and become afraid, it is easy to sink into anxiety and worry. Jesus tells us to fix our eyes on Him so we can stay above our circumstances and allow His power to be manifested. Panic makes us sink, but faith lifts us up. God wants us to learn through our difficulties that faith and His presence bring peace.

### Faith as small as a mustard seed

In Matthew 17:20, we are assured that a small amount of faith is all it takes: "I tell you the truth, if you have faith as small as a mustard seed, you can say to this mountain, 'Move from here to there' and it will move. Nothing will be impossible for you." In this passage, Jesus says that even a small amount of faith can bring the impossible. When we put our trust in God, we no longer act in our own power, but surrender to His. And His power is greater than any power we could ever have or encounter. Jesus wants us to get a grasp of this so that we can believe in His promise to work on our behalf.

The message of Christ is, do not give up. Perhaps circumstances are not working out as you wish and the answers to your worries have yet to be seen, but that is the life of faith—believe when there is nothing in the natural to believe in. It is this belief in the goodness, grace, and power of God that eliminates worry.

### Finding Confidence in God

When you feel worried, talk to God (prayer). Brain scans and EEG monitors verify that prayer and meditation change the brain for the better! In his research at the University of Pennsylvania, neuroscientist Dr. Andrew Newberg found that prayer and spiritual practices reduce stress and anxiety. Furthermore, when God is thought of as good instead of punitive, anxiety is reduced.[3]

The apostle Paul reminds us that God is always with us. That alone should cause us to stop worrying. We are never alone. Peter also tells us to cast our cares on God, to pray about everything, and to leave worry behind. To cast our cares on Him means to allow Him to work.

In his commentary, Matthew Henry says, "To cast our burden upon God is to stay ourselves on his providence and promise, and to be very easy in the assurance that all shall work for good." Henry goes on to say that if we do this, God will sustain us and supply our needs.[4]

Our difficulty in casting our worries on God has nothing to do with Him, but everything to do with how little we think of Him. Like Job, if we do not understand the person and power of God, we reduce Him to our level, incapable of acting on our behalf. What results is a lack of confidence in Him. And this lack of confidence or trust, steals our joy.

Worry is a natural part of a life based on self-effort and doubt about God. When we are the masters of our own destinies, there is no room for God to act or direct. This is a worrisome thing. However, a relationship with Jesus is an open invitation for those who are weary and exhausted from worry to come and find rest. We serve a God who tells us that we do not need to labor to be at rest. He has already done the work. Our job is to come to Him and give Him our cares. Stop striving and allow God to work.

The mistake made in some circles of the modern church is to believe that faith in God brings a life free of trouble. Scripture is clear that *when,* not *if* we have trials, they build our faith and we are to rejoice. Okay—now we are really challenged! Take joy in our trials? James tells us, yes, rejoice, because the testing of our faith brings perseverance. Even if you are not at the rejoicing stage yet, do not doubt God. Behind worry lingers doubt. Doubt says He cannot be trusted. Worry is doubt, a failure to trust Him.

**Everything is possible to those who believe**

Worry also denigrates the power of Mark 9:23. Jesus said to the man who asked Him to heal his son, "Everything is possible for him who believes." In this passage, the father is at the end of his rope with a son who is possessed by an evil spirit. A compassionate Christ asks the father how long he has dealt with this. The father answers by telling Jesus, since childhood. Then the man asks Jesus to help if He can. To this, Jesus responds, "If you can?" and follows with the statement above, "Everything is possible for him who believes." The response of the father is, "I do believe; help me overcome my unbelief."

In times of difficulty, Jesus says, come to Me. He wants us to believe for the impossible but has grace and mercy as He sees our struggle of unbelief. If you desire to believe God and take Him at His word, cry out right now and ask, "Help my unbelief." Jesus will meet you where you are.

His grace is sufficient, and He wants us to hope in Him. Our resurrected, powerful God can do anything.

Jesus punctuated the importance of faith as a way to curb worry. Mark 11 is a picture of how faith combats worry. The chapter begins with the triumphal entry of Jesus to Jerusalem. As He made His way through the town, the people shouted, "Hosanna! Blessed is he who comes in the name of the Lord!" It was a glorious moment but Jesus knew this moment would soon give way to His crucifixion.

The triumphant ride ended at the temple. There, Jesus entered, observed what was going on, and then left with His 12 disciples to go to Bethany. The next day, a hungry Jesus spotted a leafed-out fig tree hoping He would find fruit on it, but He did not. The tree was barren, out of season for bearing fruit. His reaction to this tree was to curse it: "May no one ever eat fruit from you again" (verse 14). Putting this odd moment in the context of where Jesus had been and was about to go helps understand its significance.

Jesus came from the temple where the religious leaders of the day gathered. When He returned to the temple after cursing the fig tree, He cleansed the temple and drove out those who desecrated the sacred place. The fig tree represented the barrenness of the religious system He encountered in the temple before and after His time of hunger.

Instead of spiritual nourishment, the people were trying to earn salvation and God's favor through human effort and self-will. Jesus used the fig tree to teach His disciples about the role of faith, not self-effort. Self-effort does not calm the soul or feed the spirit. It creates a type of striving that ends in frustration and emptiness.

The next morning, when Jesus and the disciples again left the temple, they passed by the tree Jesus had cursed. Peter pointed to the tree and exclaimed that it had withered away. And Jesus responded to His followers by saying,

> Have faith in God...I tell you the truth, if anyone says to this mountain, "Go, throw yourself into the sea," and does not doubt in his heart but believes that what he says will happen, it will be done for him. Therefore I tell you, whatever you ask for in prayer, believe that you have received it, and it will be yours (verses 22-24).

Asking and believing are the keys to moving any mountain in our lives. The mountain of unbelief stands in our way of letting go of worry. When we believe that God is working on our behalf, we do not have to worry. We are in His hands, and this belief creates faith, not worry.

### Climate change: from worry to hope

Perhaps the most helpful thing we can do to let go of worry is hold on to hope. My pastor used an analogy that helped me understand the importance of hope when worry comes knocking at my door. He talked about players on a football team. During a game, each play is designed to score a touchdown in order to win. But every play does not end in a touchdown. Sometimes the play is broken up or miscommunicated, the opposition steals the ball, the ball is dropped. But the players do not give up when the play does not work. They do not walk off the field discouraged and say, "Forget it. We messed up. The last four or five plays did not work. Let's just concede the game."

Instead, they stick to the game plan, knowing what brings a score. They have faith in the playbook and know that careful execution will eventually bring a touchdown. Teams that win are full of players who do not give up when the game gets tough.

Football is like a life of faith. There are times the enemy wants to steal our joy, oppose us, and break us down so we give in to despair and anxiety. But God says, Hey, keep working the playbook. Stand on My promises. They work. Believe that you can win the game. I told you the ending and you will be victorious. Hold on to hope and stay in the game.

Hope in God. Knowing He is powerful allows you to stay in the game until you conclude—as Job did—that God is good. The death of Christ was not the end. Satan was defeated, and Christ conquered sin and death. The power of the resurrection lives in us through Christ. This is why hope is always with us. There is reason to be optimistic.

Scripture also tells us that love makes faith work. Galatians 5:6 says, "The only thing that counts is faith expressing itself through love." First Corinthians 13 concludes by linking faith, hope, and love together, but elevates love to the top. With faith, we can move mountains, but without love nothing is accomplished. We have a heavenly Father who loves us and wants to give us good gifts. Do not stop contending for all God has for you just because circumstances look grim. Believe He loves you unconditionally and will bring something good out of a difficult time.

At the core of a worry-free life is belief. As we put our trust and faith in God and believe in the resurrection power and His plan and purpose for our lives, we can live a life that not only pleases God, but also brings contentment. Once we believe, we can learn to take our thoughts captive and bring them to God.

❧

Bottom line is this. From a spiritual perspective, trust in God is rooted in a belief that God loves us, is for us, and wants our best. His grace meets us where we are. At the same time, His presence and love for us motivates us to change and be more like Him. When we attack our unbelief and trust God's love for us, we can move the mountain of worry.

## Worry-Free Exercise

**BODY:**

Prayer and meditation change the brain. Contemplate a loving God and note the effect on your physical body.

**SOUL:**

Reflect on this sentiment by Henry Ford: "I believe God is managing affairs and that He doesn't need any advice from me. With God in charge, I believe everything will work out for the best in the end. So what is there to worry about?"

**SPIRIT:**

Evaluate where you are in the process of believing that God is managing your affairs. To help unbelief, meditate on Mark 9:23.

*Everything is possible for him who believes.*

Ask the Lord to help your unbelief, accept His grace, and trust His love.

Chapter 6

# What to Do with
# Worried Thoughts

*Worry is a cycle of ineffectual thoughts*
*whirling around a center of fear.*

**—CORRIE TEN BOOM**

In the previous chapter, we briefly covered the role of our beliefs as they relate to worry. We discussed how worry, at its heart, is born out of unbelief. If we do not trust God and ask Him to help our unbelief, we will stay stuck in worry.

### Worry-free living is more than positive thinking

Next, we want to look at the role of our thoughts in maintaining worry. Worry does not go away by simply thinking good thoughts. Eliminating worry requires more than positive thinking. Jesus speaks to us at a deeper level. We are to work on our thoughts and learn to take them captive, remembering that the heart of winning the worry war is to believe the truth about God. Believe in spite of the evidence of the moment. Believe when circumstances look grim. Believe when there appears no answer to a problem. Believe when you need an answer and cry out, "Lord, help my unbelief!" He will and does.

Once we believe in the goodness of God, we can tackle our thoughts. Worried thoughts create worry. Remember the study published in *Clinical Psychology and Psychotherapy* that concluded that 85 percent of the time our worst fears never materialize?[1] Think about this. Time and energy are spent worrying about things that will most likely never happen. And the more we dwell on worried thoughts, the more those thoughts feel real and repeat in our brains.

### THE LESSON FROM WHITE BEARS

Consider the classic study of white bears reported years ago in the *Journal of Personality and Social Psychology*.[2] A group of researchers showed a movie about white bears to two groups of people. One group was told *not* to think about white bears and the other group was given no such instruction. The group that was told *not* to think about white bears actually thought about them more than the group that was told nothing. In other words, trying not to think of something specific made people think of it all the more.

When we apply this to worry, we learn that the more we try not to worry, the more we do. Then we dwell on those worried thoughts and they stay in our mind. Telling yourself not to worry is like telling yourself not to think about white bears.

Since trying to stop worried thoughts does not work, what about trying to suppress them (push them down)? In an earlier chapter, I mentioned that this tactic actually leads to anxiety. Here is why. A worried thought enters your mind. The more you try to suppress it, the more aware you are of the unwanted thought. It is as if the brain searches for the very thought you are trying so hard to suppress, like activating the search mode on your computer.

In the process of trying not to think about the worried thought, you might try to distract yourself. But whatever you think about during the distraction then gets linked to the worried thought. This creates more connections to the worried thought in your brain—and the worried thought returns and is now associated with more thoughts and experiences. Thus, efforts to suppress and distract yourself from worried thoughts make them more difficult to resist. The fight against worried thoughts may actually strengthen them! Suppressing worried thoughts does not work.

## Identify the worried thought

So what do you do? Identify the worried thought. Let it come and then identify it. What are you thinking right before you feel worried? It is most likely a negative evaluation of yourself or the situation. A thought like "I can't do this," "I'm inadequate," "I will fail," "People will make fun of me" usually precedes worry, so it is important to identify what comes in to your mind.

We have already learned that false beliefs prompt worry. The more we believe worry serves a purpose (for example, it distracts us from the reality of the moment, motivates us, and so on), the more we worry. We also learned that in to order to give up worry, a first step is to stop that believing worry serves a good purpose. Once we discard the belief that worry is useful, we can then focus on truths about God (for example, He can be trusted).

Now we can identify specific thoughts that cue worry in our everyday lives. Since worry is a habit we want to break, we begin by identifying which thoughts trigger worry.

It works like this: Something happens (we have a thought or experience). That thought or experience triggers worry. For example, seeing a car crash on the interstate is an experience that can trigger worry. Having a thought about being late to work can trigger worry. Watching the nightly news is an experience that can trigger worry. Or wondering what the biopsy will show is a thought that can bring on worry.

*Negative thought or experience* ⇨ *WORRY*

When we have a negative thought or negative experience, we need to pay attention to it. Even though a thought or experience triggers worry, we may not be aware of what that thought might be.

When I treat people with anxiety problems, they often tell me that no thought precedes their feelings of anxiety. This is not true. They have a thought but have yet to identify it. So the key is to be more aware of what you think or feel *before* you worry. If you struggle to identify the negative thought that precedes worry, use this chart to help you.

| Example situation (What is happening?) | Emotion (What are you feeling?) | Worried thought (What are you thinking?) |
| --- | --- | --- |
| Talking to boss | Anxious | I know he hates me. |
| At the dentist | Anxious | I can't tolerate the pain. |
| Husband leaves the room | Worried | He wants a divorce. |

Worry is cued by automatic negative thoughts. When those negative thoughts are not dealt with, they develop into a worry habit. Here is an example. A negative thought runs through your head: *What if I don't make it in time for work?* If you decide to dwell on that thought, it becomes worry. The more you think about this negative possibility, the more worry grows.

*Negative thought* ⇨ *WORRY* ⇨ *HABIT*

**Take the thought captive**

To break the worry habit, as soon as you identify the worried thought—for example, *What if I don't make it in time for work?*—answer the thought with a more reasonable or realistic thought. *I will deal with it*, or *My boss might get mad but I can explain what happened*, or *I can't control traffic and I will have to take the consequences*. In other words, counter the worry thought with the confidence that you can handle the uncertainty or problem of the moment. And even if you cannot, reassure yourself that the world will not fall apart. Answer the thought with confidence that you will tolerate and survive the situation.

Now add another column to your chart:

| Situation | Emotion | Worried thought | More reasonable thought |
|---|---|---|---|
| Talking to boss | Anxious | I know he hates me. | He is probably under stress. |
| At the dentist | Anxious | I can't tolerate the pain. | Relax. I can do this. |
| Husband leaves the room | Worried | He wants a divorce. | Ask him if he is mad at me. |

Notice I added a column entitled "More reasonable thought." In order to think of a more reasonable thought, you first acknowledge the worried thought and take it captive. This is the prescription given in 2 Corinthians 10:5. Captivity implies not allowing a thing to have free will or a mind of its own. When something is taken captive, it loses the freedom to wander where it wishes.

Taking our thoughts captive means not allowing them to wander where they wants to go, in this case to worry. The thought is under your control. You can dwell on that worried thought or take it captive and bring it into obedience to Christ. To do so means to voluntarily check the thought according to the mind of Christ. Is the thought in line with God's Word? Is it reasonable for the moment? Are you basing this thought on anything real or only on imagined things? Are you assuming the worst?

In the examples above, the worried thought is taken captive and replaced with a more reasonable thought. The worried thought is replaced with a new thought based on truth and grace.

Paul affirms that our thinking matters. In the spiritual world, the mind is a battlefield. It is the place the enemy can taunt us with doubt, negativity, discouragement, and lies. According to 2 Corinthians 10:4, the weapons we use to fight negative thoughts do not come from our own power. It is through the power of Christ in us that we can take thoughts captive and stop negativity in its tracks. Our weapons include the defensive armor of God that we put on daily (Ephesians

6:12-18—peace, faith, truth, and so on), the Word of God, prayer, and the power of the Holy Spirit in us.

Our natural mind does not automatically go to the things of God. We need the Holy Spirit in us to renew our mind. This transforming of the mind, which Paul speaks of in Romans 12:2, is the key to becoming worry free. As our mind is exposed to the truth of God, we are humbled by the work the Spirit does in us—changing us from the inside out. His truth rids us of lies associated with worry. His truth builds our faith and provides hope. It replaces lies and distortions with truth.

So back to the example, *What if I don't make it in time for work?* This worried thought is in my mind. I take it captive by grabbing it and telling it not to wander in worried waters. I control where it goes and bring it to Christ. Practically speaking, I take a thought that is born of wounding, lies, or trauma and make it more reasonable.

### Seven thought patterns that lead to worry

Worry is often dependent on certain negative thought patterns that contain inaccuracy, irrationality, or distortions. For example, mind reading is a thought pattern that leads to worry and should be avoided. If, for example, worried Peggy says to herself, "I know my boss is going to be mad at me for being late," but then the boss says, "Okay, Peggy, I understand about traffic. Try not to let it happen again," the evidence speaks for itself. Peggy cannot read minds. No one can, and attempts to do so only engage people in worry.

Specific thought patterns that lead to worry must be recognized and corrected. In order to do so, become aware of your inner dialogue of self-talk. Let's review a number of thought patterns associated with worry. Use this list to help identify what might be operating in your self-talk.

### 1. Jumping to conclusions

Jumping to conclusions is a thought error associated with worry. It involves forecasting a negative outcome and assuming it is a foregone conclusion before it ever happens. For example, "My child will be off the soccer team if he misses practice." In this parent's mind, the foregone conclusion is that the child will be off the team. In reality, the child's dental appointment ran late and he missed practice, but the coach did not remove him from the team. The parent jumped to a conclusion and worried for no reason. The conclusion anticipated did not come true. So what did the worry do for that parent? Nothing but make her miserable. Did jumping to a conclusion help anyone? No, it simply made the atmosphere tense until the coach responded.

## 2. All-or-nothing thinking

Another common thought pattern is all-or-nothing thinking. This involves thinking in absolute terms rather than thinking about all aspects of a problem. It is living in black-and-white with no shades of gray. All-or-nothing thinkers split the world into *always, never, every,* or *none.* For example, "*Every* time I go to the doctor, he finds something wrong with me." This thought causes worry for any upcoming doctor's appointments. In truth, the last two times this person was at the doctor, minor problems were found. All the other visits were fine.

But the thought error is to divide experiences into two camps— *every* or *none.* There is no middle ground. Because the doctor found problems once or twice, *none* does not work so *every* is the only other possibility. However, it is not. This is a thought error. Doctor's visits may or may not turn up a problem and a person cannot predict which time this may or may not be true. Uncertainty is involved. Worry comes in because the person is convinced that a problem will be found based on all-or-nothing thinking.

## 3. Overgeneralization

Jim was upset that his stepdaughter had seemed cold and distant during her last visit. Because there was ongoing tension in their relationship, Jim assumed she hated him. He worried about future visits, thinking he would never win her over. This was an overgeneralization. She was still grieving the loss of her parents' marriage. Her loyalties were divided between her father and Jim. Visits were tense because of recent loss, not because the stepdaughter hated Jim. Healing takes time.

Getting to know Jim would ease some of the tension for the

stepdaughter. She did not hate him. She hardly knew him and that made her visits uncomfortable. And yes, she was a bit angry about the divorce. This was normal but was not a sign of hating the new man in her mom's life. Jim's thought that he was hated was an overgeneralization. He ascribed the tension to hate. Not so.

Overgeneralizing is when you have one bad experience and then think it will always be the same. In Jim's case, the negative interaction with his stepdaughter led him to overgeneralize. The stepdaughter was not excited about Jim's presence but she did not hate him.

### 4. Disqualifying the positive

Worriers have an amazing talent for shooting down positives and focusing on one negative possibility. Sarah did this as a way to guard herself against hurt. Her boyfriend was uncertain about their relationship and broke up with her. His reason was that he needed more time to date around. Sarah was only the second girl he ever dated. He felt the relationship was getting too serious too fast.

Sarah took the breakup hard and began to worry that there was something wrong with her. She was too sensitive, too pushy, too intense, and so on. The more Ron, her ex-boyfriend, tried to assure her that those things were not true, the more Sarah was convinced she was flawed. Ron listed several characteristics he loved about Sarah. It did not matter. Every positive Ron told her she shot down.

Sarah took the breakup to mean she was flawed and nobody wanted her. Ron's attempt to dispel this notion went nowhere because she continually disqualified every positive thing he said. Sarah worried that being flawed meant she would never find a boyfriend. The drama was based on her thought error of disqualifying the positives.

### 5. Overestimating a negative outcome

Just because something negative happens once does not mean it will happen every time. For example, if you fail an exam, do not panic. This does not mean you will fail every exam and eventually have to drop out of school. But someone who overestimates the outcome thinks that one failed test will lead to expulsion.

### 6. Magnifying or catastrophizing

You probably know the expression "Making a mountain out of a molehill." That describes the thought error of magnification—taking something small and making it bigger than it really is. We also call this *catastrophizing*. This type of thought error leads to exaggeration of a threat, which then leads to worry. This was Cheryl's problem. She had one bad interaction with someone in her church. That experience led her to believe the church was an unsafe place, and she worried about going back. Her thought was, "I can't handle going to that church."

One person in a church does not represent everyone in a church. But Cheryl was convinced that her bad experience had been too traumatic to allow her to return. Her discomfort over the possibility of seeing the woman who had upset her in the sanctuary or running into her in the hallway was too much. She made a mountain out of a molehill. She took a conflict and made it a war!

However, the church was large. Cheryl might not have ever run into this woman again. Better yet, Cheryl could have confronted her and told her she had been hurt by what happened. The issue was a small thing. To leave the church based on one interaction, thinking the church was unsafe, was based on catastrophic thinking. A negative interaction is easily fixed by a conversation, not by running away and worrying about safety.

### 7. Emotional reasoning

Emotional reasoning is when you allow feelings to hijack your thinking. If something *feels* like it will happen, you believe it will. You ignore the objective issues involved. Pam's son missed his curfew and emotional reasoning took over. Pam told her husband that she felt something terrible had happened. She noticed several car accidents reported on the nightly news. She was sure their son had been in one of those accidents even though no one from the police or hospitals had called.

She was worried sick. Her husband could not calm her down until their son came through the doorway. it turned out that his cell phone had died and traffic was backed up on the freeway. He knew he would be late but was unable to notify his parents. Pam had focused on all the horrible things that could be delaying him. A traffic tie-up was not one of the possibilities. She was thinking with her emotions and did not engage her head. She ignored clues that did not support her conclusion.

At times, we have an intuition that is spiritually based. It is prompted by God. But thinking rooted in irrational fear and anxiety can run our thoughts and make us so anxious we can hardly function. There is a balance between emotions and thoughts that must be sought.

In general, negative thought patterns lead to discomfort and anxiety. Worry impairs clear thinking and use of good judgment. Worry also maintains a negative focus that can lead to physical symptoms and avoidance of situations.

Finally, worried thoughts elevate safety over personal satisfaction and growth. Are we willing to sacrifice a meaningful life for a safe emotional life? That is what happens when worried thoughts rule the day.

**Become a problem-solver**

Problem-solving is different from trying to anticipate all the problems that could arise from a situation. Anticipating every possible negative outcome only leads to worry about what has not yet happened. Problem-solving focuses on the moment, takes a concern, and moves it to action. In order to curb worry, answer the negative thought or experience by becoming a problem-solver.

*Negative thought or experience* ⇨ *PROBLEM-SOLVING*

For example, Randy received a phone call from his ex-wife. She informed him that she was suing him for more child support. The phone call triggered worry in Randy. He already felt stretched beyond what he could afford. How would he be able to pay more? Money is a real concern, and Randy was tempted to worry. He could allow worry to emotionally paralyze him. His ex-wife was the worry prompt, and conversations with her ended in worry. That was his past pattern.

But he had a choice. He could worry about a lawsuit, obsess on his lack of money, and dwell on his anger at his ex-wife. Basically, he could choose the path of becoming stuck in worry.

Or he could listen to what his ex was saying and decide to go another route. He could problem-solve. He asked his ex-wife why she wanted an increase in child support. She did not answer the question but yelled and told him she and the kids deserved more. He tried to redirect the conversation back to the specific request. The ex-wife still did not answer and belittled him and called him names. Randy then told her he would hang up the phone if she could not have a reasonable conversation regarding her request. He was trying to understand her thinking. The ex-wife ignored him and continued to berate him. Randy ended the conversation since it was going nowhere. He then called his lawyer and told him to prepare for a lawsuit. The lawyer assured him that he would get on it immediately and that he saw no cause for an increase in child support.

Randy took a concern that presented itself and engaged in problem-solving. First, he tried to talk about the request. That went nowhere. Then he called his lawyer for legal help since the issue was a legal one. *His choice was to not engage in worry, but to act on what he could.* His action did not stop his ex-wife from being rude and unreasonable. It did not prevent more cost for legal fees, but it did stop him from worrying about what *might* happen in the future.

Randy's action required one more step: to grab his negative thoughts about his ex-wife and deal with them differently. If he chooses to think about how unfairly she behaves, how rude she is, how often she name-calls and makes unreasonable demands, he will be angry. Despite his efforts to work out an amicable divorce, she will not cooperate. That is a reality he must accept. The situation is what it is, and no amount of worrying is going to change her lack of cooperation. What he can control is whether or not he allows bitterness and unforgiveness to take root.

### Redirecting thoughts and feelings

At the same time Randy accepts the reality of his relationship with his ex-wife, he can push for change by not allowing her to manipulate him. He takes charge of his reaction, the only part he has control over. He cannot control his ex-wife's outbursts, and worrying about them does not help. He must accept that he has an ex-wife who tries to make his life miserable.

What he can change is how he deals with his ex-wife. He takes action and refuses to dwell on the negativity of the moment. He redirects his thoughts of anger and upset to the action he takes: "This is the way she behaves. I must accept this but can change my response to her and not give her so much power in my life." He recognizes that the ex-wife's actions trigger the potential for worry but chooses a different path. He grabs his thoughts, stops them from going the worry route, accepts what is, and focuses on what he can control. Then he problem-solves a solution.

**When problem-solving isn't possible**

What about times when there seems to be no solution? Take for example Sarah's daughter, Ali, who has a severe peanut allergy. Ali's school has instituted an allergy protocol to follow in case she is exposed to peanuts. At the beginning of the school year, the staff used problem-solving to anticipate allergic reactions. What Sarah cannot control is exposure from children who do not conform to the ban.

Ali's classmates were warned to keep peanuts out of the classroom because of how harmful they are to her health, but kids do not always comply with instructions. Sarah could become a nervous wreck and worry every day that her daughter might be exposed to peanuts. Sarah has a choice. She has done everything possible to control Ali's environment. Every day that Ali leaves the safety of her home and goes to school is an opportunity for her mom to worry. Sarah could choose to think about all the possible ways Ali could be exposed to peanuts that day. But she chooses not to go down the worry path.

Each day, she tells herself, "I have done everything I can to protect my child in an open environment. Now I must trust that she will be okay. Yes, something could happen, but my worrying about it will not change what could be." Sarah is grabbing those what-if thoughts and accepting the reality of the situation. She focuses on what she has done to make the school safe.

⌘

In order to accept what is and push for change, we must balance emotions with reason. We must let go of the idea that we can control every bad thing and accept things as they are. At the same time, we use problem-solving to change what we can. We take negative thoughts captive and renew them with truth. Accept what is, and intervene when you can. This delicate balance of acceptance and change is what keeps worried thoughts from running our lives. In a later chapter, we will spend more time discussing the concept of acceptance with change.

## Worry-Free Exercises

**BODY:**

When you engage in anxious thinking, relax your body and engage in deep breathing or progressive muscle relaxation until you reduce physical tension.

**SOUL:**

1. Identify the thought behind the feeling of worry. (Use a chart like the one on page 88 to help you record this process.)

2. Identify negative thought patterns you may be using.

3. Generate a more reasonable way to think about the issue that does not include distortion, irrational thought, or thought errors. Rehearse the new thought or renewed thought.

4. Keep a diary of worried thoughts and expected outcomes. At the end of the day, evaluate whether that worry came true. Make a note about the actual outcome.

5. At the end of the week, check to see how many worries actually came true.

6. Decide if the evidence supports worry.

7. When you engage in a negative thought pattern that leads to worry, ask yourself these questions:

a. Is there evidence that this is true?

b. Is this always true, or are there times of exceptions?

c. Has this been true in the past—every time?

d. How true is this? What are the odds of it happening again?

e. If it happens, what is the worst outcome possible?

f. Are my emotions running my thoughts?

**SPIRIT:**

Daily, renew your mind.

Meditate on Psalm 139:23:

> *Search me, O God, and know my heart;*
> *test me and know my anxious thoughts.*

And on Romans 12:2:

> *Do not conform any longer to the pattern of this*
> *world, but be transformed by the renewing of your*
> *mind. Then you will be able to test and approve what*
> *God's will is—his good, pleasing and perfect will.*

Chapter 7

# Health Worries

*Don't chain your worries to your body. The burden
soon becomes heavy and your health will give too
much of itself to pick up the extra load.*
—**ASTRID ALAUDA**

One day last summer I was reading the morning paper, enjoying my coffee, when I came across a small article tucked in the health and wellness section of the *Wall Street Journal*. According to research in a British medical journal, calcium supplements, typically used to prevent osteoporosis, could be linked to an increased risk for heart attack. Great! I put down the paper, looked at the three calcium supplements in my hand that I was about to ingest, and wondered, "Now what? Do I take the calcium, phone a friend (or maybe a doctor), or simply worry that I am killing myself?" (Ah, the thought of a worrier!) Forget the fact that I am still confused about whether the coffee I am drinking is good or bad for me. Now I have calcium to add to the list of health worries! Reading the results of that study got me thinking about the health habits of my family. The kids are not getting five servings of fruits and vegetables a day, no one sleeps the recommended seven hours a night (I have teens), and who is drinking eight glasses of water a day? Should I be worried?

Thanks to newspapers, blogs, websites, chat rooms, talk shows, and other ways of obtaining health news, we are inundated with new findings along with their implications. Pay attention and you will end up confused and feeling like your family gets an F in health. The abundance of information and prescriptions for healthy living can set worry into motion.

If you find yourself yelling across the table, "Get your hands away from that steak! You are going to have a heart attack!" you may need to practice the relaxation methods suggested! Seriously, we need to be careful not to allow the plethora of medical information available to make us crazy.

We can literally worry ourselves sick. There are so many things that *could* go wrong or *could* happen in the future when it comes to our health. Some things we have control over, and many we do not.

### Expect the unexpected

With no history of back problems, I found myself sitting in a neurosurgeon's office reviewing the results of a recent MRI. Yes, an MRI. Six weeks earlier, I had noticed minor symptoms but dismissed them.

It was the spring of 2004—I was in the beginning stages of writing another book. As I sat at my computer each day, I noticed increasing pain in my right hip. My initial thought was that the pain came from sitting in an uncomfortable chair for several hours each day.

As the pain intensified, I decided to take regular breaks—walk the dog, roll on a therapeutic ball, kneel at my desk, and move around more often. My husband even bought me a better chair, thinking that might solve the problem. Nothing seemed to make a difference and the pain grew in intensity.

I called my chiropractor, who also specialized in alternative medicines. She gave me a few natural supplements to help with inflammation but told me to see my internist and a pain specialist. The pain specialist tried several approaches and treatments. Each provided a few hours of relief, but then the pain would return with a vengeance.

At this point, I was unable to sit and could only stand or lie flat in bed. The pain was unbelievable, like nothing I had ever experienced. Even the pain of childbirth did not compare, as this pain never relented. My leg felt like it was on fire, the numbness was impacting my ability to walk or stand, and I was relegated to bed 24/7. Pain medications were prescribed, but I am highly sensitive to any medication and could not tolerate any of them. In retrospect, I believe this was a blessing, as I would have taken anything to make that nonstop pain go away. I remember thinking, "This is how people become addicted to pain medications."

I could not sleep or place my leg in a position to stop the pain. I was confined to bed for weeks while my family reorganized life without me. Mostly, I cried and prayed.

During this time, I had to cancel a graduation party for my husband, who had completed his PhD. Determined not to miss the graduation ceremony, I was taken to the event lying down in the backseat of our car. Once at the site, I lay prostrate on the lawn and watched him walk across the stage. As soon as the ceremony was over, I was taken home and put in bed again. My life was confined to my bed, and the pain was constant.

I worried I would lose my sanity because the pain was so great and I was exhausted by it. All I could do was write and pray. I propped my laptop on my bed, lay on my stomach, and wrote a book that, ironically, became a bestseller. The distraction was what I needed to stay sane. As I focused on the writing, I could get through the day. I wrote an entire book in eight weeks! But the nights were terrifying because sleep was nearly impossible.

I called out to God in my distress. I was totally dependent on Him to give me the strength to endure the pain and keep my sanity. During those days, His presence was strong and I knew He was with me. It was the only thing that kept me going. As I prayed for God to help me endure this ordeal, He did.

The days blurred but somehow I got through them, gutting out the pain until a plan could be developed. The mystery to me was how this had happened. As I reviewed my history trying to come up with clues as to what was causing pain, I thought of a few things that might have aggravated my condition—travel in planes, hauling book boxes from airports, long car rides to visit family, and—oh yes, a terrible fall on the ice six months prior.

Growing up, I had been an ice skater. During a Thanksgiving visit to my hometown, I took my kids to the ice rink that held so many after-school memories for me. Thinking I was 14 again, I attempted a flying camel and fell on the ice so hard I could not move. My daughter watched in horror as she saw me paralyzed on the ground. The pain was excruciating, and I thought I had seriously broken something and would be taken by ambulance from the rink. Because my daughter was with me and I did not want to scare her, I downplayed the pain and eventually managed to get up and get back to my parents' house. As I recalled this incident, I wondered if something had shifted in my back that day.

The pain specialist decided we needed to be more aggressive. Treatments were providing only temporary relief and were not addressing the root cause of my symptoms. He was also concerned that the pain now radiating down my right leg was causing numbness in my foot. Next step was an MRI scan.

Stretched out on my back on the MRI bed, I remember thinking, "What am I doing here? I have no history of back pain and was able to resume life six months ago after the fall. It feels like this pain came out of nowhere." It did not! The scan clearly showed the source of the problem. I was scheduled to see a neurosurgeon. Talk about the unexpected!

If you have ever been delivered medical news you do not want to hear, you know the shock and fear that can grip you in an instant. The test results indicated a huge bulge on L5 (one of the lowest vertebrae) that could only be fixed through back surgery. The bulge was pinching my sciatic nerve. If I did not have surgery immediately, I risked becoming incontinent with permanent nerve damage. I heard the words but sat there stunned. Back surgery? People I knew considered back surgery only as a last resort after years of treatment. Even then, results were mixed in terms of fixing back problems. For a moment, I felt fear. But I knew God was with me. All those hours in prayer had heightened my awareness of His presence.

I left the neurosurgeon's office in a daze. Meanwhile the pain continued and I did not think I could endure it even another day.

I live on a cul-de-sac with four physician families as neighbors. We are a friendly bunch of people who regularly get together over food and fellowship. So when I heard my only option for pain relief was back surgery, I took my case to the neighbors. Every one of them looked at the MRI and agreed with the neurosurgeon. There were no options they could see. I took this as confirmation to proceed with the surgery and had a peace about it.

The week before the surgery date, many people prayed with me for healing. I knew God was capable of moving that bulge off the nerve and healing me. I had no doubt. And then something happened.

The night before I was scheduled for surgery, I was suddenly pain-free. After six weeks of unremitting pain, I was sitting in my family room rejoicing! I could move, sit, and dance around the room without pain. My first thought was that I could cancel the surgery in the morning. But that thought was short-lived, as the morning brought a return of the pain. It was even more intense. However, that momentary relief provided me the first night of sleep I had had in a month. God gave me rest to prepare me for the surgery. Yes, I was disappointed, but I was grateful for the break from pain. I would have preferred healing without surgery, but God knew the path I must take.

The next day, I prepared for surgery. We prayed, and I was at peace. Despite the pain, I knew God was working on my behalf. The surgery went well, and when I awoke in the recovery area, I was overwhelmed by the presence of God. To this day, I cry just thinking of how close He felt in that recovery room. It was as if I touched a part of heaven. His presence was so strong, I was laughing. I wanted to shout out His goodness, but I was too groggy to speak.

The peace I experienced was not something that can be manufactured. It was perfect and supernatural, and it had the ability to calm my body, soul, and spirit. It was the delivered promise of God—His presence with me through the trial.

The recovery was long and not easy. Gradually I began to re-engage life while I worked with a physical therapist. Today, I am considered a back-surgery success. The experience taught me how to endure a time of suffering with God by my side. It also gave me a compassion for those in physical pain and a deeper insight into the power of addiction.

During pain and disease, God is present. The secret to my endurance was calling on His name, the name that was acquainted with grief and suffering. His presence is what causes worry to evaporate and brings peace to painful and troubling experiences.

### Be careful with self-diagnosis

Information is power, and we have an abundance of it on the Internet. The problem is how we use that information. Trying self-diagnosis can lead to incorrect diagnoses (this happens more than you think). I have done it myself. I correctly diagnosed a family member with gout using Internet websites. Tests by the doctor confirmed this. But then, I incorrectly diagnosed the cause of leg pain and worried about nothing. On the Internet, you can find a disease or illness for almost any ache or pain. Those of us who are not physicians can easily make incorrect diagnoses and recommend wrong treatments. We can also worry because, based on inadequate advice and training, we think we have a serious problem.

If you spend any time reading blogs, you will come across people with no credentials doling out health advice. Be careful when you diagnose yourself, and always back up your opinion with medical expertise. I have treated people who spent lots of money on false cures and faddish treatments that have no scientific basis. As an example, think about all the fad diets that promise to melt the pounds away or liquefy cellulite. The old adage applies here: If it is too good to be true, it probably isn't.

Media regularly report what is healthy and what is not, as I mentioned earlier. The information changes based on new studies and replication of findings. Drugs are determined to be safe by the FDA and then recalled years later because of fatalities. Not too long ago, a prescription medication that was on the market for five years and had been taken by approximately two million people was removed due to risk of heart attacks and stroke. Even though we have in place national safeguards regarding the safety of drugs and medications, additional research can change recommendations. But if you stay up nights wondering about drug safety, you won't get much sleep. It is not possible to anticipate every side effect and problem. A certain amount of risk accompanies medications and treatments.

## Worry gone wild

Aided by regular access to information, worrying about health can become an obsession known as hypochondria, a psychological condition in which any physical symptom is interpreted as a serious medical problem. Even in the face of no evidence, a hypochondriac believes he or she has an illness. Doctors, friends, and families cannot convince such a person to think differently. For the hypochondriac, a sore throat is throat cancer, a headache is a brain tumor, a fainting spell means diabetes, and so on. This form of excessive worry often requires professional help from a mental-health provider.

Taylor is an example of a hypochondriac who needed mental health treatment. She was convinced she had a brain tumor because of regular headaches. After visiting several doctors who diagnosed her headaches as stress-related, she continued to search for a doctor who would order a scan of her brain. She believed she was very ill.

Following several medical workups finding no physical cause for her symptoms, Taylor refused to believe that her headaches were psychologically based. She was sure the doctors overlooked important information and would discover evidence of a tumor if her brain was scanned. Her obsession led to expensive testing and uncontrolled worry.

It is normal to be concerned about symptoms when you first notice them. For instance, if I notice a mole that looks irregular and odd, I have it checked by a dermatologist. If it is shown to be of no concern, I do not worry. But a hypochondriac like Taylor dismisses the evidence and worries.

Often excessive health worry is prompted by traumatic events, such as the death of a father by heart attack at an early age or witnessing a death in a car accident. Other times, health worries can grow out of less dramatic experiences. During a certain period, I remember seeing a number of fortysomething women in my therapy practice. They had all been diagnosed with breast cancer. At the time, I was in my early forties, and the constant talk about the disease and the toll of the treatments left me anxious about my own body. Anxiety was heightened because of the exposure I had to so many women battling cancer.

### Worry over side effects

Even if you do not turn mild symptoms into serious disease, it is tough to be completely anxiety-free about your health. All you have to do is listen to one of myriad drug commercials that spell out a host of possible side effects. After hearing the litany delivered at record speed, it is a wonder any of us ever takes a medication!

Drug companies are required to list side effects of their medications. This is a responsible thing to do, but it certainly can send a worrier into orbit. Just think of all the things that could possibly go wrong or happen to you just by taking a drug! That is why you must weigh the pros and cons of taking any medication. And if you decide to take a prescription, pay attention to your body but do not let your mind wander into worry. Be armed with information to make decisions, but do not allow that information to cue anxiety.

## Common health worries

Because health information is so readily available, you would guess that most health worries would be easily dispelled. Not so. Myths about health can grow when information is not accurate but is broadly disseminated. Myths are based in a lack of knowledge; other times, they grow from outdated facts. In some cases, health myths are promoted to scare us and create worry so that we will buy products or consume goods. Here are a few of the common health worries people accept that are based in myth, not science.

### Toilet seats: carriers of disease?

In the world of Internet health, toilet seats get a bad rap! In truth, they are not as likely to spread infections or disease as you might think. Most people wash their hands after using the bathroom and thus reduce the risk of spreading bacteria and disease. And it is *not* true that toilet seats can infect you with sexually transmitted diseases, a common myth.

So wash with soap and water and refrain from touching your hands to your mouth before you scrub away, and you can avoid most germs that cause problems. In fact, the toilet seat is probably more sanitary than the public surfaces you touch after you leave the stall.

### Am I safe when I pump gas?

Another common worry involves fumes released while pumping gas. People fail to realize that pump hoses have special nozzles that trap most vapors when you are refueling. Thus, fumes from pumping gas are not considered harmful. You may be sensitive to their smell, and you should wash your hands after pumping gas, but worry about the vapors making you sick is a worry that will not materialize.

### What about doorknobs?

Have you ever been in a public restroom and wondered about the doorknobs? A healthy habit is to wash your hands and kick the door open or use your elbow to open the door. That way, you avoid transferring germs from public surfaces to your mouth or eyes, should you touch one of those areas after you wash your hands. Maybe that sounds a little Monk-like (meaning the neurotic hero of the TV show, not the spiritual guys). It might be, but as noted above, there are germs in those public spaces that can go from your hands to your mouth or eyes. You can also use a hand sanitizer after you leave a public space. You can take reasonable precautions without obsessing over the possibility of germs making you ill. Although you are exposed to many germs in a day, you have built up immunity to more than you know. You can be wise without becoming worried.

### Toxic nails?

Women often ask if nail salons are toxic places. If you walk into one and smell the chemicals in the air, it may mean the salon is not well ventilated. Should you worry about this? Maybe, but alarmist reporting does not help us decide whether our concerns are real.

Consider this headline: "Toxic Nail Salons: Why Your Polish Color Could Be the Next Agent Orange."[1] Nail polish compared to Agent

Orange! The article goes on to say that chemicals in base and top-coat polishes have been linked to cancer, birth defects, and skin rashes.

But what does the research say? An investigation at the University of Texas's Anderson Cancer Center in Houston found exposure to UV light in the salons to be more of a concern than the polishes used. Whether the exposure to UV nail lamps is enough to make you worry is questionable.[2] But upon further investigation, Dr. Roshini Raj, an assistant professor of medicine at New York University's medical school, tells us in her book *What the Yuck? The Freaky and the Fabulous Truth About Your Body* that using nail lights every week or two could add up to significant UV exposure.[3] Thus, along with toxic chemicals, UV light could add to your worries.

So should you never frequent a nail salon? If you are pregnant, you may want to skip the manicure. Otherwise, investigate the facts about topics like this and make informed decisions. Worry comes with ignorance, engaging in risky behavior, or both. And in some cases, the jury is still out.

### Die from hair dye?

If you dye your hair, you may worry that the chemicals in hair dye put you at risk for cancer. According to the National Cancer Institute, over 5000 different chemicals are used in hair dyes, some of which have been shown to be cancer-causing in animals. However, a review by the International Research Agency for Research on Cancer (IARC) concluded…"personal use of hair dyes is not 'classifiable as to its carcinogenicity to humans.'"[4] This means the group could not say *with certainty* that hair dyes produce cancer in people.

Hair dyes used before the 1980s were more carcinogenic (cancer-producing) than newer dyes. A study found that women who used hair dyes before 1980 had a 30 percent increased risk of non-Hodgkin's lymphoma (NHL) compared to those who had never used them. But the risk was removed after the hair dyes were changed in 1980.[5] With information like this, you can err on the side of taking no chances, make an informed decision with the information you know, or risk it. What you do not want to do is worry over every product used.

## What about radiation from microwaves and cell phones?

Finally, what about the health risks of using your microwave to cook? As of now (and remember, health research changes with continued research), do not abandon microwave cooking. The high levels of microwaves are contained within the oven and do not pose a health risk, according to the American Cancer Society. The same is believed to be true about cell phones, although more research is being conducted on their use by children.[6]

Usage guidelines are provided until we know more about the impact of appliances and technology on the human body. Specific instructions such as to not use plastic containers to cook with or stand close to the microwave door while cooking are good suggestions to follow while more information is learned. And remember, concerns about cancer are only one area that researchers address in regard to health anxieties. Other health concerns may take years of study to understand.

## Putting health worries in context

Now…if you are anxious and already checking the list of possible dangers to your health, press pause and breathe deeply. Here is my point: You could make a long list of all the possible things that could create problems. As we noted, health information changes regularly as research is conducted and new information is learned. If you allow every health concern to morph into worry, you will always be anxious and live in fear. And keep in mind that health reporting in popular media does not always mention limitations of research designs in applying results to the general population.

A way to guard against allowing health worries to consume you is to listen or read the information and put it in context. For example, it is interesting to note that anecdotal records of people who live long point to genetic programming as the most important variable. And that is not something in your control. With genetic inheritance, you get what you get. In part, that is why we see, for example, a lifelong smoker live to the ago of 100. Good nutrition, exercise, and other good health habits contribute to longer life, but genetics can trump it all.

How many times have you met people who practice a healthy lifestyle but have high cholesterol or heart disease? Typically, this is because of genetics. Now do not use this as a reason to throw in the towel and say, "Why bother if it is genetic roulette?" Healthy living reduces risk. However, it is not a guarantee against all health problems. And as with all the sources of worry, health cannot always be controlled and predicted. There is an amount of uncertainty we must accept.

To curb worry, remind yourself that one research study does not provide a law for how to live your life. Many factors go into sound health recommendations. And if you are not perfect in keeping recommendations, it does not mean something terrible will happen to you. For example, if you miss a few days of sleeping at least seven hours, the only danger to your health is that you will probably be irritable! The general guideline about sleep is meant to help you develop a healthy lifestyle and give your body the rest it needs to operate well.

Recently, my 90-year-old father and I were talking about his health. He has type 2 diabetes, and his blood sugar fell to a dangerously low level the other day. Had he not gotten intervention, he could have died. When I told him how worried I had been (yes, I am working on this!), he calmly said, "Hey, I have to die sometime." He meant it. He is not worrying about every drop or rise of insulin. He has lived a long life and refuses to allow diabetes to be a source of worry. He does his best to follow the guidelines, and he exercises every day. Beyond that, he leaves the rest to God.

### HEALTH WORRIES AND DOCTORS

Health worries typically pop up before, during, and after a doctor's visit. Reality is difficult to avoid when you have a checkup. Worry over test results is common. Most people breathe a sigh of relief when reports are in and results are good. But keeping a worry-free outlook when a symptom or test result is of concern is not so easy.

I remember a few years ago when my neighbor found a lump in her breast. Several tests indicated it could be cancer. In order to combat worry, she had people pray with her on a regular basis and asked God for His peace. Daily, she controlled thoughts of doom and gloom and chose to trust God and remain positive. She was amazed at how He helped her handle several reports of bad news without allowing anxiety to overwhelm her. Thankfully, in the end, there was no cancer. However, the lesson she learned was to trust God even in the face of bad news and not allow negative reports to consume her.

## When the situation seems impossible

In my own life, a diagnosis led to years of worry that seemed impossible to overcome. As I mentioned in a previous chapter, I endured seven years of infertility. When my husband and I decided to begin our family, nothing in either of our medical histories indicated this would be a problem. About two years in to the process, I decided to see a fertility specialist. If there was an issue, we needed to correct it to achieve a pregnancy.

After a month of painful testing, the results showed no medical reason why we were not getting pregnant. We were diagnosed with "undefined infertility," and I joined the approximately 7.3 million women of childbearing years unable to have a baby.[7] I was devastated. Not only did I not expect this, but we were given no explanation why this was happening.

The months and years that followed were a true test of my character and faith. I struggled to go to baby showers of friends. I found myself irrationally angry with new mothers wheeling their babies through the mall. When Mother's Day arrived, it was impossible to sit through the church service without breaking down in tears. I could hardly bear working with clients who were unhappy about being pregnant and wanted to abort their babies.

I was depressed and anxious and could not seem to pull myself out of the chronic funk that seemed to weigh down my thoughts. I knew I was not thinking straight and this bothered me. And I was not able to manage my emotions well. Some days I would burst out crying; other days I felt strong.

I had no history of depression, but I felt I was coming clinically close to losing it each month. Every month, I was hopeful but then devastated.

My body became my enemy—unwilling to function as it should. I submitted to painful and humiliating testing and procedures that yielded no results. I worried that I was becoming self-absorbed and obsessed with an unreachable goal. The more I tried not to think about infertility, the more I did. Infertility was always on my mind, and I hated that!

During that time, seven of my friends were also struggling to get pregnant. We did what most women do and formed an informal group to support one another. Through the months and years that ensued, all of them eventually got pregnant and delivered babies. It was bittersweet. I knew their pain, and many of them had medical causes of their infertility that required surgery and painful treatments. But I was now a group of one…and my dream of being a mother was fading.

I remember sitting in choir one evening listening to a woman talk about going through infertility for two-and-a-half years. I was thinking, "I could never do this for that long. God, please do not make me endure this even another year." A few months later, I was pregnant but then miscarried. It was devastating.

And in the middle of this chronic stress, I encountered friends who must have taken their cue from Job's friends in the Bible story. I am sure they were well meaning, but their attempts to console me were hurtful and ignorant. One person attributed my infertility to secret sin. If that was the case, it was secret to me! Daily I was before God, examining my heart, as I was acutely aware of needing to be right with God.

Others tried to tell me that pregnancy eluded me due to pride in my life. Really? I wanted to drag those who held this notion to my doctor's appointments and put them in a gown, allow interns to poke and prod them like cattle, and then let them tell me how prideful they felt! Infertility is humiliating and erases any pride left in a person.

And then, of course, there was the contingent of believers who attributed it all to lack of faith. The irony of this was that faith was all I had. My defense was to know my Bible and talk to sensible people who understood that faith does not eliminate suffering.

I followed the advice of every doctor and research finding, and even crazy advice from friends. I found myself standing on my head, practicing stress reduction, and tracking ovulation. Like a chronically ill patient, my life was organized around getting pregnant. Honestly, it was exhausting.

Finally, after years of angst and failure, I gave up and surrendered to God. Nothing I did had worked. Reality hit hard. I felt I had two choices. I could become angry and bitter and live in anxiety or give the entire ordeal to God. I ended the fight where I should have begun—total surrender to God with a decision that His plan for my life was good and filled with purpose and that He would work all things for my good. It just took me years to come to this conclusion!

I began to fast and pray, "Not my will, but Yours." If I was not to give birth, let the desire pass. My age was now becoming a factor. Doctors warned me that my eggs were getting old, possibly contributing to the problem. Great—not only was I not conceiving, but my eggs were old. What do you do with that kind of information? But I was at the point of acceptance now and quietly took these concerns to God and placed them in His hands. Here are my desires, my old eggs, and my life.

Then one day I turned to a verse in Psalms. Psalm 92:14 reads, "They shall still bear fruit in old age; they shall be fresh and flourishing" (NKJV). As soon as I read this, I thought about my old eggs and felt God was telling me, *Do not worry. You will bear fruit that will be vital, fresh, flourishing.* I closed my Bible and felt at peace. Anxiety left. I knew God was up to something.

The rest of the story is filled with miraculous moments and God restoring the lost time. He gave me two beautiful children, even in "old age." Once I submitted to His plan and timing, worry took a backseat. I finally recognized God's grace operating in my life, and I knew I had to trust Him or give in to depression and doubt.

In my case, the story ended with two children. This is not always the case, but the process of dealing with infertility requires total surrender to God. And I believe that was the point. God used seven years of struggle to teach me how to be at peace when I do not get the results I want. He taught me to trust Him when I see no reason to do so. And

He taught me how to lay down worry on a daily basis. These are lessons I am still learning.

Health issues have a way of bringing us to a point of trust and dependence. They often test our faith and show us what we truly believe. Difficulties and pain can be used to bring us to the awareness of our need for God. As with Job, there may be no explanation for our suffering, but there is opportunity to bring glory to God through it.

∽

In sum, there is fine line between becoming too relaxed about personal health care and obsessing over it. Somewhere in the middle is balance. We do what we can to take care of our health. We listen to information as a form of help and wisdom, but we avoid the temptation to worry over every daily finding. This is not easy to do, as mentioned, especially when health awareness is so prominent in our culture.

We can worry about possible health problems. We can complain when our bodies do not work the way we would like—or we can learn to live with the uncertainty of disease and deficiency. Despite the fact that we live in a fallen world, God still heals and walks with us through pain. His promise is to be with us no matter what. And that certainty is where we put our faith.

## Worry-Free Exercise

**BODY:**

Schedule a physical if you need to. Take care of your body. See a doctor you trust to give you accurate information and do what you can to stay healthy.

**SOUL:**

Write down your health worries.

Is there data to support these as realistic, or are they based on myths or Internet findings?

If they are realistic, are you doing what you need to do to take care of your body, or are you obsessing on things out of your control?

**SPIRIT:**

Surrender your health worries to God. Place them in His hands and allow His peace to fill your heart. Meditate on Philippians 4:7:

> *The peace of God, which transcends all understanding, will guard your hearts and your minds in Christ Jesus.*

And Psalm 46:1:

> *God is our refuge and strength, an ever-present help in trouble.*

Chapter 8

# Job Worries

*The reason why worry kills more people than
work is that more people worry than work.*
**—ROBERT FROST**

Browsing through a number of online news sites, I noticed numerous stories about people who had recently lost their jobs. A Kansas City blog caught my eye. Readers posted their job loss comments. Most were trying to make it through another day. Worry was a definite theme.

Rose had brought in a steady paycheck for 22 years, working for the same company. Over the past six years, she has been fighting to get disability for her husband. He now lives in a nursing home, and Rose needs her job to afford to live. A few weeks ago, she was laid off. She worries that she will lose everything.

Cathy insists she lost her job because she sounds like actress Kathleen Turner, whose voice her former boss does not like. It took eight-and-a-half weeks to receive her first unemployment payments. In the meantime, she informed her creditors and tried to make small payments to show good faith in paying her bills. But the red tape of waiting for agencies to communicate with each other left her disgruntled and frustrated. Even though she is actively job-hunting, her family depends on her, and she is worried about being hired again.

An electrician who was laid off often this past year realizes that money is coming up short to cover the family bills. They have cut costs wherever they can, borrowed from their 401K to pay property taxes on cars, and used all their savings to pay bills during dry spells. Even though they are preapproved for a home loan, there is no way they could buy a house and make payments right now. To add insult to injury, creditors are raising the interest on their credit cards even though they have never missed a payment. This man needs the economy to turn around and start hiring again, but he is powerless to make things change. He worries that all his efforts to tighten his belt and be responsible will not be enough to make it through this difficult economic time.

Another man is working in sales while trying to jump-start his own business. A meeting was called late on a Friday afternoon. Employees were informed that they were now going to be paid only on a commission basis. He is worried. How will he have the cash to cover the transition?

The stories go on and on. Regular people struggling to make ends meet in an economic downturn and plagued by worry and unrest. Jack was no exception. The atmosphere at work was tense. For weeks, he had not been eating or sleeping well. He complained to his wife that he felt tired and achy. It seemed like he was constantly on edge and irritable with his family. His concentration was poor, and he needed over-the-counter drugs for an upset stomach.

At work, morale was low. Management had made several changes that had resulted in an increased workload for most of Jack's team. Despite his hard work, Jack was having difficulty meeting the new expectations. He began to worry, knowing his bosses were scrutinizing productivity.

His wife noticed the changes in his sleep and convinced him to see his doctor. After careful examination, the doctor asked, "How are things at work, Jack?" "Not so great these past few months," he answered. "I'm expected to do the work of three people since the last layoffs. My workload is so heavy I can't even take a bathroom break! Honestly, I worry if I can keep up this pace. I used to think that if I worked hard, that would be enough. But now that doesn't guarantee anything. Management is acting strange. They are making decisions I do not understand. I worry about what is going to happen at the company."

The doctor knows that chronic job stress has set off an alarm in Jack's brain. His nervous system and hormones are working overtime. And the fact that the stress is ongoing keeps his body in a constant state of arousal, which results in physical wear and tear. Jack needs to make changes or be at risk for injury and disease.

He is not alone. According to a survey by Northwestern National Life, 40 percent of workers report their jobs to be "very" or "extremely" stressful, and one-fourth of employees see their jobs as the number-one stressor in their lives.[1] Health complaints are a common side effect of job worry.

### Challenged or stressed?

It is one thing to be challenged on the job and another to be chronically stressed. Challenges motivate and energize us, but too much challenge can result in stress and damage to our bodies.

When challenges are met, we feel satisfied. When demands are not met and satisfaction gives way to worry, the line is crossed. And when people feel there is too much stress, they are more often absent and tardy, reports the Bureau of Labor Statistics.[2]

So when it comes to worrying about your job, determine if your work challenges have become a source of stress. If you feel expectations are beyond what you can do because of lack of resources, time, or personnel, stress results. If you are losing motivation to do well because you feel overwhelmed, it is time to pause and make changes. Too much job stress can zap your energy and leave you physically and emotionally spent.

The signs of job stress include low morale, apathy, and negativity; becoming cynical, bored, anxious, tired, frustrated, depressed, alienated, irritable, and angry; wanting to miss work; and experiencing more physical problems like headaches and stomachaches.

In order to reduce stress, first determine the source. Is stress related to you and the way you behave, or does it have more to do with working conditions? Or is it both that are contributing to on-the-job worry?

### It's me, not the job

When thinking about work stress, consider this. What *you* feel is stressful may not be stressful to someone else. This is because your unique personality and coping styles influence how well you handle job stress. For example, if you are easily frustrated, things that do not bother other people may irritate you. If you struggle with change and your job involves constant change, the demands may be too much—the job may be better for someone who can adapt quickly to change. If you have problems with authority, taking orders from a boss you do not like may rub you the wrong way and create ongoing tension. If competition bothers you and you prefer to be a team player, a job built around competition can be unsatisfying. If you are easily bored, then a routine job will quickly frustrate you. You will probably be bored if you are a creative type and your job involves repetitive tasks. These are just a few examples illustrating how important it is to work in jobs that fit your personality.

Coping on the job also relates to personality traits. According to Purdue University researcher Daniel Mroczek, chronic worry, anxiety, and depression are associated with the personality trait *neuroticism*[3]—a trait that is often studied in psychology. *Neurotic* describes someone who experiences negative emotional states such as anxiety and depression more than the average person. When stress hits, people who score high on this trait tend to respond poorly and see their situation as difficult and threatening. They worry more than the average person and often feel something is not quite right. So someone who has this personality trait must find a way not to allow negativity to dominate his or her thinking, especially when it involves coping at work.

### Do you fit the job?

*Job fit* is a term that refers to your abilities or desires and a job's attributes or demands.[4] Your abilities can be thought of as your personality—the skills and mental ability you bring to the job. Your desires have to do with the goals, needs, interests, and value you give to the job. Matching a job to who you are is important to your performance and well-being. When you find a job that fits with your innate abilities, you do better.[5] So know yourself—how you feel about change, what you can tolerate, what excites you, how you cope with stress, and so on. Use that self-knowledge to pursue jobs that fit you.

In order to better assess job fit, ask this question, "Can I do the job?" Concern (not worry) may be warranted if your job is too taxing or above your competency level. You may need to consider a change in your job specifications, more education, or a job that better matches your training and expertise.

Next, think about your interest in your current job. People do better in jobs they care about and like. Furthermore, does the job fit with your values and contribute to your development as a person? Finally, is the work environment acceptable? If you constantly worry about your safety or health, a change may be in order.

### Work relationships

Work environments are like families. Some people rub you the wrong way; others remind you of that difficult family member. Still others are irritating and like to create drama no matter what. At work, we are surrounded by people we may not choose to socialize with, but with whom we have to find ways to get along. In this respect, we can worry about being liked, promoted, chosen for assignments, criticized unfairly, and a host of other interpersonal issues.

If you find yourself thinking too much about a co-worker or boss after hours, chances are you have allowed that person to get under your skin. Go ahead and vent to someone you trust, but then let it go. Do not allow worry to steal your time of relaxation. Do not give co-workers or bosses that much power in your life. You have control only over how you respond. You cannot control how fair, sensitive, demanding, or perfectionist someone may be.

#### LEAVE WORK AT WORK

Several years ago when I was interning at the Veterans Administration hospital mentioned, I was assigned to the inpatient psychiatric ward. My unit consisted of suicidal, homicidal, and psychotic men. The work was so emotionally intense that it was difficult for me to come home and shift gears to be with my husband. I worried about the patients, the families, the unit, and so on. The job was consuming too much of my time and energy away from the hospital.

My husband made a rule that helped bring balance to my job. I could debrief for ten minutes each evening. After that, family and relaxation were the focus. This was the best advice. I learned to vent for a few minutes and then leave work at work. We still follow this rule. It is too easy to bring work home or worry and obsess over any number of work-related issues. Balance is needed.

Your job is disposable. Your health and well-being are not. Therefore, it is important to exercise self-care. Self-care refers to you taking care of you. Take breaks, lunch hours, and vacations. You get a better perspective on job concerns when you step away for an hour, a day, or more. If you have vacation time, use it. The break will do you good.

## Five proactive steps to get rid of on-the-job worry

### 1. Organize the clutter

If you are often running around your office like the White Rabbit in *Alice in Wonderland*, thinking, "I'm late. I'm late, for a very important date!" you may need to declutter. You control your workspace. Organize it so that clutter does not add more stress to the job itself. Clutter can create distraction. Distraction slows you down, which can cause you to miss deadlines or turn in late assignments. And somewhere in all that mess, you may have something important to work on that you have forgotten about.

It is amazing how clearing papers off your desk can clear your head. Or how organizing files and putting things where they belong can reduce stress. When things are in order, you can find what you need quickly, minimize distractions, and move faster on the job.

## 2. Find positive, supportive people

Find positive, supportive people in the workplace. There is probably one person who will give you a lift in conversation and help you stay positive on the job. Make sure you befriend that person. Better yet, be that person for other people.

## 3. Use humor to break tension

If you could have one of the best antidotes for stress, would you take it? If I told you it is something you can easily access and is free, would you want it? If I raved about how this one thing does everything from decreasing the risk of heart attack to stimulating the immune system, would you order it? Well, get ready, because it is something you already have. (At least I hope you have it.) It is humor!

Now if you do not have a sense of humor, go get one. Read joke books, listen to comedy, and learn to laugh at funny things. You are probably taking life too seriously and need to laugh at yourself and others at least once in a while.

My colleagues in my private practice group used to kid me about my therapy sessions with clients. They could not hear our talk through the soundproof walls, but the sound of laughter escaped through my doorway. They wondered what was going on that was so funny. Let me assure you, we were dealing with painful and difficult subjects, but I always found some way to bring humor into the mix. Why? Humor reduces stress.

Humor is a self-care tool that fosters a positive and hopeful attitude. It releases emotions and stimulates the immune system.

Humor takes a stressful condition and turns it into a challenge. Studies at Cornell University found that people exposed to humor in the workplace were not only more creative problem-solvers, but they could also better see the consequences of their individual decisions. Humor defuses stress and makes it easier to look at a situation and do something about it. And it is fun. It feels good to laugh, and laughter does wonders for the physical body.

I'm not suggesting you laugh off serious matters. Do not deny or avoid problems. But if you can maintain a sense of humor, it helps cut tension and brings people together instead of creating division. Try it.

### 4. Lose the perfectionism

One of the signs of being a perfectionist is being dissatisfied with your work. Perfectionists worry about every detail on the job. They worry about getting the approval of the people with whom they work or disappointing others. Frequently, they ask for extensions on deadlines in order to keep making changes toward perfection.

Perfectionists must work on their thoughts regarding task completion and making deadlines. For example, missing a detail will not cause the world to end. Perfectionists think it will! The temptation to obsess over every detail must be examined and re-examined. Worry about job details does not change a thing, except ruin your health and work experience.

Perfectionism impacts productivity and job satisfaction, and it can damage relationships with supervisors and colleagues. It is self-imposed stress. Thus, a balance must be reached between doing a job perfectly and being indifferent about the outcome. The middle ground is a job well done.

Letting go is most difficult because it requires a lowering of perfectionist standards. A few ways to practice letting go include arriving at work on time instead of early, leaving when you are scheduled to be finished for the day instead of working late, allowing a bit of a mess on your desk, or determining a specific number of corrections before turning in an assignment. Try making a few of these changes. They will reinforce the reality that on the job perfectionism is not needed.

If you or your boss is a perfectionist, look at the big picture and do not get lost in the details. Once you have completed a job, do not look back and second-guess what you have done. Move on and keep moving forward or you will get stuck in the details. If you need help overcoming perfectionism, a mental-health professional can aid you through a type of counseling called cognitive behavioral therapy.

### 5. Evaluate your working conditions

Working conditions matter in tackling job worry. If they are poor, there may be very good reasons to be concerned. For example, if you work in dangerous conditions, the possibility of an accident is real. Take this into consideration when you address worry. If you choose to work in dangerous and unsafe conditions, make peace with that choice, or make changes. Use the following questions to evaluate your work environment.

In your place of work, are there...

- too many hats to wear or a workload that is too demanding of resources and your time?
- infrequent breaks and long hours, including shift work?
- multiple tasks that have little meaning or are done in a hectic manner?
- few or no indications of control or direction?
- conflicting and unclear expectations?
- inflexible work hours?

Does management...

- exclude workers from decision-making?
- evidence poor communication?
- lack feedback and support?
- show no recognition for good work?
- rarely encourage worker development?
- appear unfriendly to family policies?
- lack resources to do the job?
- have poor leadership?
- not make provision for growth or advancement?
- push rapid change with little support?
- allow dangerous physical conditions such as crowding, noise, air pollution, or ergonomic problems and not value safety?

## Handling job uncertainty

Juanita was worried about losing her job. Her company was downsizing, and people were being laid off. Because she had little interaction with her boss, she had no idea what she thought about the layoffs. Rumor was that people with the biggest salaries were on the chopping block. Juanita had been with the company for years and received a good salary.

Every night, she called her friend and obsessed over the possibility of being laid off. Finally, out of frustration, her friend told her to be assertive and talk to her boss. Ask how decisions were being made and if there were more layoffs coming. In other words, "Juanita, do something proactive instead of worry."

Juanita mustered up the courage to talk to her boss and was pleasantly surprised. She found her open and willing to discuss how layoffs were being decided. Juanita learned that there was a decision-making system unrelated to salaries. By the end of the meeting, she was relieved and understood more about how upper management operated. She refocused on the task of leading her team. Her energy was now directed to helping the company through the downsizing.

Job uncertainty is a stress that can paralyze anyone. The act of worrying about losing your job creates health problems worse than actually losing your job. University of Michigan sociologist Sarah Burgard found that people who constantly *thought* about losing their jobs were worse off in their health (and in one study, also more depressed) than those who had *actually lost* and regained jobs. The data showed that worry over job loss was a predictor of poor health, worse than the impact of smoking or high blood pressure!

Since there is such a powerful physical impact with worry over job uncertainty, how do you deal with worry when job uncertainty is high? Sometimes, simple reassurance fixes the problem. That was all Juanita needed. But she had to ask for it.

When you do not trust the direction of your company, doubt develops. There are times when simple reassurance corrects this. Other times, doubt is dispelled by building trust so you are not trying to read someone's mind or acting according to rumor. Even when the outcome is negative, trust helps you handle it. When we trust someone, we understand why he did what he did and believe it was not motivated to hurt us.

Now what if Juanita had been given bad news? Her assertive move could have resulted in this discussion: "Juanita, you heard right. We are laying off people with the highest salaries, and you are in line for a layoff." At least Juanita would know the direction of the company and could plan to look for another job. Even bad news can eliminate worry if you accept reality and realize there is nothing more you can do about it.

Regardless of the outcome, Juanita could choose to stop worrying and focus on her next step. Worrying didn't contribute to finding a new job or performing her current job. Worry only agitated her and diverted energy needed to do her best. The antidote to worry in Juanita's case was trust—trust that she could have an honest conversation with her boss so she could problem-solve her next move.

When there is no trust and job uncertainty remains high, ask yourself these questions:

1. Can you be certain about everything in life?
2. Do you tend to become negative when things are uncertain? Is there a positive possibility or outcome as well as a negative one?
3. Can you live with the fact that your job is uncertain? If the likelihood of losing your job is high, can you know this and not allow it to consume your thinking?

The point is, worry does not make job uncertainty go away. However, it can paralyze you and result in poorer health. So when job uncertainty is causing you to worry, be assertive and see if you can get more information in order to plan your next step.

### *Ways to help uncertainty*

As in Juanita's case, work environments will always hold some level of uncertainty. But there are things you can do to increase your value to a company or in a workplace. Rather than worry about uncertainty, focus your energy on these actions:

1. *Be someone who is seen as indispensable.* The more valuable you are to an organization, the better your chances of staying. Be that go-to person.

2. *Make sure the right people know how you contribute to the organization.* For example, if you are the only firefighter who is trained on special equipment, make sure your bosses know this about you. If no one else in the salon can work with difficult customers, let the boss know you can keep those customers happy and coming back.

3. *Contribute to the bottom line of the company*—whether that is generating revenue, referrals, services, or something else. Companies like to see results. Prioritize your time on activities that get results and contribute to the vision, profit, or promotion of goods and services.

4. *Ask to be challenged.* Be seen as someone who wants to grow and be active. If you appear bored and tired on the job, people notice. I remember when I did an internship at a Veterans Administration hospital. So many of the people employed appeared to be going through the motions, with no joy or excitement for their work. It was rather depressing. Many had settled into a routine and lost their creativity and challenge. This, in my opinion, was reflected in patient care. People need a challenge to stay motivated to do good work. But the system provided no incentives for people to be creative or grow.

5. *Get along with management, especially your supervisor.* At some point in your work or career, you will happen upon a boss you do not like. Make it a point to be congenial, respectful, and cooperative despite your personal feelings. Although you are not getting paid to have a lovefest with

the boss, you are getting paid to do a job, so make efforts to get along with bosses and management.

6. *Be a low-maintenance employee with a positive attitude.* Without much thought, I could name names of people who constantly created drama at the workplace and made life miserable for co-workers. Do not be one of those people! Stay positive, look for the upside on negative situations, and do not complain or whine.

7. *If you put in extra time, make sure your superiors notice.* When that project deadline approaches or someone needs extra help and you put in extra time and effort to get the job done, let those who supervise or manage you see your willingness to step in and help.

8. *Be a team player,* always ready to pitch in and get the job done.

9. *Show an interest in learning and growing in your craft or skill.* Be a lifelong learner of your craft, skill, or work area. People who stay current with trends, research, and new ways to do things and who pay attention to how to improve what they do are valued.

10. *Be proactive and not a complainer or whiner.* Give solutions. No one likes to work with someone who always complains but offers no solutions or leadership. Stop blaming people, finding fault, or whining about problems. Instead, offer ways to improve, new methods of doing things, smarter ways to operate, and strategies to make conditions or products better.

## Handling job loss

Dan came to work ready to meet the challenges of the new corporate structure. To his complete surprise, his supervisor called him into his office and told him his job was being cut. The news hit Dan like a brick. Waves of shock and denial overwhelmed him. He cleared out his office and left, still in utter disbelief.

Weeks after the news, Dan felt himself reeling from feelings of anxiety, depression, and anger, and wondering what he could have said or done to change the company's mind. Maybe if he had worked harder, talked more to management, made himself invaluable, and so on. These thoughts would give way to anger, then shift to sadness.

He felt like he was watching a movie of someone else's life. The job loss took weeks to fully sink in to his thinking. At first, he was paralyzed and did nothing. Once the shock wore off, the uncertainty about a paycheck, career, and unemployment raised feelings of panic and anxiety.

In order to cope with growing worry, Dan had to make a change in the way he approached this loss. He stopped the what-if thoughts and decided to write down his concerns about the future. Which concerns were real? Once he decided, he was able to think of two or three quick action steps he could take to move out of his place of inaction.

An important step in moving forward was not holding on to the anger he felt. Even though Dan knew his boss had to release him, he harbored unforgiveness toward him. That unforgiveness affected Dan's mood and spiritual life. So he prayed, and made a decision to forgive and trust God for the future. No matter how unfair the layoff felt or even was, Dan was the only one who could go out and get a new job. As he took the necessary steps, he had to be careful not to give in to hopeless thinking or feelings of rejection. And it helped to exercise, eat better, and do volunteer activities while he was looking for work.

Finally he came to an acceptance of the loss and was able to create an entire action plan. The many emotions associated with job loss resurfaced at times, but he refused to give in to worry. The key was to work through the emotions and not get stuck in them. Some days were better than others. Eventually, Dan was ready to face the work world again with confidence and a positive perspective.

When someone loses a job, it helps to understand that their accompanying emotions are similar to grief. Feelings of shock, denial, anger, sadness, bargaining, and acceptance cycle in and out while the grieving process is in full gear. During that time, a few action steps make the process easier. One action point is to call one person who will listen and help connect you to an opportunity. At the same time, begin researching one ideal employer and learn as much as you can about that organization and how to position yourself for employment. Search for meaningful connections based on former work experience, education, charity work, church, or hobbies. Social media sites can help with those connections. Seek out someone who will help you practice answering tough interview questions such as, "Why did you leave?" or "What was your biggest weakness?" The point is to not allow worry to paralyze you.

**Finding balance**

I mentioned the need to take a break from work and find balance in your life. When senior executive candidates were surveyed, the findings revealed that they were reluctant to apply for senior positions because of concerns they had about pay and their ability to maintain a healthy balance between home and work responsibilities.[6] Those candidates were looking at their lives holistically and asking, would promotion be worth the added worry and strain on their mental health and family? This is an important question—one we should all ask. How much are we willing to jeopardize other parts of our lives (health included) just to make more money or be promoted?

Hopefully, you will value balance in your life enough to let go of worry and establish boundaries between work and your personal life. There are times when passing up a promotion makes sense. Taking care of elderly parents, being available for young children, or being at home to talk through life issues with a teen are reasons to say no to more time constraints, money, or power.

If you struggle with this balance of work and family or find you are so stressed that worry is taking over your life, many companies have an employee assistant plan (EAP) that can help you work through priorities and cope better with stress. Check with your human resources department to see what is available, and do not be afraid to ask for help. Your health and mental health depend on it.

## Worry-Free Exercise

**BODY:**

Take time away from work. If you have vacation time, use it. Do not bring your work home with you, and take breaks during the workday to clear your head.

**SOUL:**

1. If you struggle with worry created by your job, write down your concerns.

2. Next use the practical helps in this chapter to match a strategy to each specific concern.

3. Instead of getting lost in worry, evaluate where you can make changes. Use the following list as a checkpoint:

   __ Do I have personality traits that contribute to worry (low frustration threshold, perfectionism, neuroticism, or something else)?

   __ Is my job a good fit for who I am?

   __ Is the work environment safe?

   __ Am I seen as a valuable worker?

   __ Do I leave work at work and know how to relax away from the job?

   __ Would better organization help reduce stress?

   __ Do I use humor to break work tension?

   __ Am I coping well with job uncertainty, embracing this reality but not letting it become a source of worry?

   __ (For those who have lost a job) Am I being proactive, grieving the loss but moving forward with action steps?

   __ Do I have a good balance between work and other parts of my life?

**SPIRIT:**

Meditate on Matthew 6:25-34. Trust God for today and your future.

> *Do not worry about your life, what you will eat or drink; or about your body, what you will wear. Is not life more important than food, and the body more important than clothes? Look at the birds of the air; they do not sow or reap or store away in barns, and yet your heavenly Father feeds them. Are you not much more valuable than they? Who of you by worrying can add a single hour to his life?*

> *And why do you worry about clothes? See how the lilies of the field grow. They do not labor or spin. Yet I tell you that not even Solomon in all his splendor was dressed like one of these. If that is how God clothes the grass of the field, which is here today and tomorrow is thrown into the fire, will he not much more clothe you, O you of little faith? So do not worry, saying, "What shall we eat?" or "What shall we drink?" or "What shall we wear?" For the pagans run after all these things, and your heavenly Father knows that you need them. But seek first his kingdom and his righteousness, and all these things will be given to you as well. Therefore do not worry about tomorrow, for tomorrow will worry about itself. Each day has enough trouble of its own.*

Chapter 9

# Money Worries

*If you are distressed by anything external, the pain is not
due to the thing itself but to your own estimate of it; and
this you have the power to revoke at any moment.*

—CHARLES F. KETTERING

I'm not a money expert, so this chapter is not going to change your
life in terms of investments or adding to your wealth. What it will do
is help you put money in perspective so worries about it do not consume your thoughts.

Money is a major source of worry for many of us. According to the
Pew Research Center, 35 percent of adults worry *often* about money,
and only 15 percent of adults say they live comfortably. In addition, 52
percent of adults report they have a debt problem.[1]

In fact, people all over the world worry about money. A 2009 Reader's Digest international poll asked the question, "What stresses you
the most?" "Money" turned out to be the number-one reason for stress
in most countries. Malaysia, China, Singapore, and the United States
topped the list for being the most worried about money. France, Italy,
and Russia worried the least about money and more about family issues.[2]

Now before you purchase that villa in Tuscany or the south of
France, consider the cost—but more importantly, consider your age.
Money worries peak during our forties.[3] However, as we get beyond our
forties, money worries diminish (hey—a positive for aging!). According to a recent Gallup poll, once we hit the age of 50, money worries
drop off significantly. Even though this seems hard to believe, given all

the news we hear about the plight of the elderly, it is true. Aging brings relief from money woes.

As you might guess, the same Gallup poll found that people who are employed and have incomes higher than $60,000 a year worry less than the unemployed and those who make less than $60,000. Obviously, employment and a good salary help keep money worries at bay.

Of the two sexes, remember that women worry more than men except during their thirties. Men and women who are thirtysomething worry equally about money.[4] Other than that, women have the edge on worry.

Regardless of sex, age, or salary, how we think about and use money makes a difference in eliminating worry. Money is a necessity that has to be dealt with every day. We need it to buy food and clothing, pay for transportation and housing, and meet other obligations. It is not something we can avoid, so a healthy perspective on how to use it is important.

## A biblical view of money

Money is widely referenced in the Bible. In the New International Version, the word *money* is used more often than the word *salvation*. Jesus felt money was an important topic—16 of His 36 parables deal with money. In general, we are warned not to be greedy, as the love of money can bring temptation and problems, and not to make money an idol, because the love of money blocks our relationship with God. We are to be good stewards of money, giving charitably to those in need and not storing up riches just for ourselves. And we are to avoid debt, as it can be a form of bondage.

Keeping money in a proper perspective takes planning and diligence. Our culture glorifies wealth and fortune. Money is viewed as the answer to most of life's problems. The message is that you can never have enough. Thus, both the lack of money and the desire for more money bring worry. A common worry is, do we have enough money for now and for the future?

There are broadly applicable steps you can take to lessen money worries. These steps are under your control no matter what economic conditions are. Remember, though, that our aim is to *eliminate* worry from our lives.

## Eliminating worry by controlling spending

### *Do not shop until you drop*

If you feel born to shop, you need a rebirth! Debt usually follows too much spending. And debt is a source of worry that is very real. Shopping is a very easy way to put yourself in debt if you are not careful.

Shopping can be like emotional eating. It can be used to cheer us up when we feel down. The anticipation of buying something releases a brain chemical that produces a feeling of well-being. When we feel anxious or stressed, we see the reward (an item to purchase) and the brain says, "Go for it! You will feel better." We do feel better momentarily because good feelings come when we anticipate a reward. Buying, even when economic times are tough, can lift a person's mood. In fact, psychology professor Karen Pine surveyed women and found that 79 percent would shop to cheer themselves up when in a financial crisis.[5] The very thing we should not do when money is tight, we do because it makes us feel better for the moment. Shopping, then, can become an emotional habit that lends to worry.

In order to not shop for purposes of mood enhancement, control your emotions and employ coping skills that do not include spending. When you are tempted to spend to make yourself feel better, pause, wait one to five days, and see if you still need the item. This cooling-off period gives you time to decide if you really need something or are acting on impulse.

I will never forget the sales pitch my husband and I fell for because we were pressured to make a decision immediately. It involved joining one of those national buying groups. The showroom was beautifully laid out, and we needed a number of home improvements that could be purchased at this buying company for discounted prices. It all looked so enticing. The catch was that we had to decide on the spot to join. The problem was that the monthly membership fees were steep and our contract obligated us for years to come. We were so caught up in the moment (unusual for us) that we joined. A day later we looked carefully at the terms and monthly outlay and deeply regretted our decision. Fortunately the company was kind enough to let us out of the contract for a fee.

### Identify spending triggers

Know what triggers your urge to spend. If spending is not related to true need, then the urge could be cued by any number of emotional issues, like relationship problems, job stress, parenting problems, and so on. Identify the issue that makes you feel stressed or anxious, and then choose a healthy coping strategy. For example, the stress of single parenting is overwhelming you. You decide to go to the mall just to get out of the house and take a break. You spot a dress that would look fabulous on you. You do not need it, nor can you think of where you would wear it. But it looks amazing on you and makes you feel special and cared about for the moment.

Put the dress down, walk out of the store, and call a friend. Meet the friend for coffee and treat yourself to good conversation. (Conversation and eye contact are stress reducers, and they're free.) You will feel better and have no buyer's regret later! Best of all, you did not spend money unnecessarily.

### Budget busters: impulse purchases

"This is just what I needed." "Look—it is on sale." "I deserve this." "I probably should wait, but hey, why not?" "My wife would love this." "I just want to get this and I don't care what it costs."

Familiar words?

Impulse buying is especially easy and prevalent on e-commerce sites. Tantalizing special sales, free shipping, seasonal promotions, and more pique our interest and we buy. According to tests conducted by a company called User Interface Engineering, impulse shoppers are not aware of what drives their buying online.

Researchers found that impulse purchases were driven by category links on sites and by the design of sites, not by price. Navigating a category link usually results in money spent and continued browsing.

Category links expose you to more of a site's product line and more pages on the site. Impulse buying is influenced by exposure to more products.[6] The design influences the shopper's strategy, and that strategy drives impulse buying.

Think of it like this. You need a sweater for an outfit. You walk into a store, knowing the sweaters are near the back. As you make your way through, you stop and browse through the jewelry, shoes, and scarves. When you reach the sweaters, you do not find one you like, but you find a pair of earrings and a scarf for another outfit along the way.

On e-commerce sites, you are browsing in a store. As you "walk through," you may purchase items you did not intend to buy. Browsing through products by clicking on categories encourages impulse buying.

You may be thinking you are safe from impulse buying if you stay off-line. Not so. In a 2002 comprehensive study by Shapiro and Associates for Marketing Support, Inc., of Chicago, researchers found that almost one-third of consumers make a sizable impulse buy every week. The median price of the impulse buy was $30. About a quarter of that group spent their money in specialty stores.

What motivates us to buy on impulse? Is it the gratification or lack of self-restraint? In part, yes to both, but we are also influenced by color, noise, sparkle, texture, and other qualities of an item. Impulse buying is also prompted by how uncomplicated a product appears to be and to how much we feel a personal connection to that product. Catchy displays, grouped items, repetition of an item in a store, placement of items near a register, and so on, are all part of the marketing to get you to buy on impulse.[7] As you can see, a great deal of thinking and research goes in to encouraging you to do this.

One way to curb impulse buying is to avoid malls, e-commerce sites, and multiple trips to stores. When I was doing my Apple Computer One-on-One training, the Apple store was directly across from three of my other favorite stores. So every week, before or after my training session, I would browse those favorite stores and usually end up buying something. When my training finished, my spending decreased significantly because I was not frequenting those stores every week. The temptation to impulse buy was removed.

Because shopping is influenced by factors out of your awareness, stick to a budget, exercise self-restraint, and institute a cooling-off period for purchases. The cooling-off period is especially helpful in curbing impulse spending.

### BUYING MAKES ME FEEL POWERFUL

Money is symbolic of power. In addition to boosting our mood, spending makes us feel powerful because it influences how we interact socially. For example, buying and owning an expensive car is perceived as a sign of status. A person with money can purchase an expensive home, pay for top schools, buy lavish gifts, travel, and do things people without money cannot do. In fact, just the handling and touching of money makes us feel better according to research published in *Psychological Science*.[8] The study found that touching and thinking about money can lessen pain and ease feelings of social rejection. In other words, money affects our emotions and thinking. It is concrete, something we can touch and exchange for things we want or desire.

When something feels out of control in your life, the physical act of buying can lift your mood. However, this is not a habit you want to develop. Buying to feel better or feel more powerful can lead to money woes. Celebrities like Burt Reynolds, Kim Basinger, Gary Coleman, MC Hammer, and others have filed bankruptcy after making a great deal of money. The must-have lifestyle that often accompanies wealth cannot always be sustained long-term. The feeling of power that comes with money can be addictive if one is not careful.

### Work at debt-free living

Debt creates worry. Given today's economic climate, it is easy to go into debt. For years, Americans have lived on credit and spent more than we could really afford. Eventually, debt catches up to all of us.

For some, it means foreclosure on their home, bankruptcy, or other kinds of financial hardship. Recovering from financial difficulty takes patience and planning. Along the way, worry can be your companion.

Any debt counselor will tell you that the way out of debt is to pay off credit and stop spending what you do not have. So why is it so difficult for the majority of us to follow this simple and effective advice?

In essence, debt is a result of not looking at the big picture of your finances. It builds as you react to the short term and do not consider the long-term consequences of spending. Too many people live beyond their means and rationalize spending by telling themselves, "I deserve this."

Lori is a good example. Out of college, she acquired a job with good pay. Immediately she bought designer furniture and treated herself to expensive dinners out. Her thinking was that she could pay off the furniture over time. But about four months into her new lifestyle and payments, she was falling behind on her bills. In retrospect, she wished she had not bought the furniture.

In order to live on her salary, Lori stopped the expensive dinners out, but the furniture payments were a commitment she had made for many years to come. Those purchases resulted in a tight budget. As she watched her friends take reasonable vacations and occasionally go out to dinner, she regretted her expensive furniture purchases. Lori realized (after the fact) that she had got caught up in purchasing expensive furniture at a time in her life she could not afford it and did not need it. At the time of her purchases, she focused only on the monthly payments rather than on her overall debt and expenses. The steep monthly furniture payments limited everything else Lori could do with her money. Thus, she began using credit cards to continue her lifestyle. The credit-card debt (with 18 percent interest) was putting her in a financial hole each month.

Eventually Lori cut up her credit cards, paid off her debt, and tightened her belt to make the monthly furniture payments. The sad part was that the furniture she had dreamed of having become a reminder of overspending. The joy was gone, the debt was long-term, and her lifestyle was limited.

## Do not live on credit

Lori's story is a grim reminder that credit is a dangerous animal. As tempting as it is, credit is not a solution to money problems. Pay your bills first when you get your paycheck. Then use credit only when you know you can pay off the debt that month. Even then, you take a chance because unexpected expenses can pop up, causing the credit payment to take a backseat and accrue interest.

Jake was a college student who decided to apply for a card to help establish his credit. He had little experience with budgeting. At first, he put the credit card in a safe place and did not use it. Then he hit a rough spot financially and thought, "This is why I got the card. I will only use it for this emergency." Once the payment cycle hit, Jake was short due to other expenses and could pay only the minimum amount. Because Jake was young and had no credit record, the card came with a hefty 23 percent interest rate on unpaid debt. The rollover balance cost him additional money he could not afford. Then the brakes went out on his car, and he again used credit to pay. The $800 for the brakes was not in his budget, and interest costs were building. Eventually he paid off the card but it cost him an additional $250 in interest—money he did not have to spend. He cut up the card, having decided it was too tempting.

Jake story is repeated many times a day. People use credit and go in debt. Worry comes with debt. As mentioned, the best plan to eliminate worry is to use credit only when you know you can pay it off with no penalty.

## Control what you can, and let go of the rest

If we allow it, worry about finances can be a part of our everyday life. There are always bills to pay, children to put through college, medical expenses, car and home repairs, and so on. In order to stop worrying about money, do your best financial planning and then let go of what you cannot control. Worrying does not fix a thing.

Alex was someone who had to learn to let go. She became a single parent after a troubling divorce. Her ex-husband paid minimal child support. With four children to support and a much lower budget on which to live, Alex had to sell her home and downsize. At first, she was bitter about the change and worried every day about how all the changes would impact the children.

She was an emotional wreck, but a counselor helped give her perspective. She was acting financially responsible. She was keeping her family out of debt by downsizing and doing what she could to control her expenses. She needed to focus on the proactive steps she was taking—to forgive her ex, let go of bitterness, and move on. With the help of God and her friends and with smart decisions, her family would be fine. Worrying was not helping anything and was in fact making her ill.

Two things were in Alex's control. She could release bitterness and forgive, even though she felt the divorce was not fair. Holding on to resentment and hate was eating away at her spiritually, emotionally, and physically. She had to put her trust in God, not in her ex's future actions.

The second behavior in Alex's control was moving into more affordable housing. When she did, she had to fight feelings of resentment again. Was it fair? No, but worry took her down a negative path. The move put her in a better financial situation and ended worry about how she would afford upkeep and taxes on her previous house.

Alex controlled what she could and let go of what was out of her control. The following are seven ways to do this in your own life.

### 1. Live according to your means

You may want an iPhone, a 3-D television, a new car, a bigger house, and so on. If you cannot afford these purchases, do not buy them. Control your spending and stick to a budget. Wants are not needs. Giving in to wants often puts us in worry situations. Decide what is a want and what is a need. For example, I want an iPhone, but I do not need one. And right now, with the cellular-phone plan I have, changing phones makes no sense in our budget. It may, I hope, in the future. Right now, I need to make decisions with my head, not my heart. The point is to resist spending what you cannot afford or does not make sense. (Purchase patience is especially difficult if you are an early adopter of new technology.)

### 2. Have an emergency fund

Worry is less likely when you have a backup plan for emergencies. The rule of thumb is to save about three to six months' worth of expenses for an emergency, or else have resources you can command. In reality, any amount saved usually makes people feel better and worry less. Do what you can and pay down debt.

Erin is single and does not have much money left over once she pays her bills, but she is committed to putting $50 a month in an emergency savings account. She has done this for the past three years and has saved $1800. Her thinking has been, "All I have to do to save is brew my own coffee and take it to work instead of buying it on the way to work." This one simple change was doable. Knowing that she has saved emergency cash keeps her from worrying.

### 3. Be positive

Money worries are not worth the stress. Do what you can, and plan and enjoy your life rather than worrying about what might be. Keep a positive attitude. There is always a way to problem-solve, get help, or improve your situation.

Disappointments and money problems will come, but your attitude toward financial stress makes a difference. Like me, you will probably make mistakes along the way. You can learn from bad money decisions. When you make a mistake, figure out what you did wrong. Stay positive. This is what Keith did, and his wife was amazed at how little he worried.

Keith made a bad investment based on bad advice. Once he lost the money, he refused to beat himself up and worry about the mess he had created. Instead, he met with a financial counselor, reviewed the bad deal, and concentrated on how to make better investments. He took responsibility for a bad decision, but stayed positive about his future goals. And he learned from his mistake so he would not repeat it.

### 4. When finances become a problem, get active

In times of financial difficulty, it is easy to throw in the towel and feel overwhelmed. Anxious feelings often lead to inaction, which does not change money problems. When finances are tough, take action. Meet with a community counselor, financial planner, debt counselor, or someone you respect who handles money well. That person can help you look at the big picture and determine a strategy to take the pressure off. This might include getting an extra job or a better-paying job, selling what you can, downsizing, and so on.

In addition you can attend free seminars, sign up for free money sites online, or read books about money strategies and investments. The point is to not wallow in worry but do something productive to change your situation.

### 5. Rethink your current expenses

In order to stop worrying about money, ask yourself if you can eliminate anything, redo a deal, change insurance for a better price, and so on. Take a look at all your current expenses and see if there is a way to reduce them. For example, Sharon cut several hundred dollars from her monthly budget by shopping for car insurance and better cell-phone service. Small changes make a difference in monthly expenses. Review your expenses regularly, looking for ways to save.

### 6. Plan ahead for predictable expenses

Planning ahead for known or predictable expenses can eliminate worry. Examples of predictable expenses are graduations, college, home repairs, weddings, retirement, car repairs and purchases, the birth of a child, and so on. It is easy to worry about these expenses if you have not saved or made a plan to pay for them. So for example, if you are buying a house and want your children to attend public schools, plan your purchase in a neighborhood that has good public schools. When your children begin school, it is not too early to research state-college tuition plans and begin contributions.

As children grow and develop interests and hobbies, set aside additional money to cover those activities. For example, my daughter has been in dance since the age of three. Dance classes are a regular monthly expense that must be in the budget. Dance also includes specific clothing and shoes. Pointe shoes run $70 to $80 every couple of months.

Budgeting for this is important and may require that a teen work a part-time job to help pay these expenses.

## 7. Tithe

Make it a habit to give a tenth of your income to your church or ministry. Give the tithe immediately when you get paid or you will be tempted to use it for other needs. I cannot stress how important it is to build a habit of paying the tithe immediately and not think of it as your money. I have heard story after story of people who have changed their debt picture by tithing. It sounds counterintuitive, but it is not. When God establishes a principle, it works. God asks us to give Him a portion of the finances He provides for us. Honoring that command honors God and brings blessing in our lives.

## You can't buy happiness

In sum, money worries are often brought on by spending money you do not have. The pressure to buy is intense in our culture, but remember this, money does not bring you happiness. In fact, a survey by University of Rochester researchers found that money is actually a source of anxiety. Ill health can result from trying to reach material milestones.[9]

In the study, people who focused on personal growth, close relationships, community involvement, and physical health were better off physically and emotionally than those who pursued materialism and image-related goals. Gaining wealth and admiration through financial success does not bring lasting satisfaction. Despite the emphasis our culture puts on "keeping up with the Joneses," the pursuit of money can lead to an emotionally and spiritually empty life, with worry always knocking at the door.

Although there is nothing wrong with accumulating wealth and making money, it is the *love* of money that is problematic. When money becomes the object of our affection (an idol) and not a means to an end, we create problems. Money can't buy you love, respect, or happiness…but it can buy you worry.

## Worry-Free Exercise

**BODY:**

Instead of spending to lift your mood, list other activities that do this for you. A few examples were given in this chapter—meet with a friend for good conversation, employ a cooling-off period before buying. List several other activities that would help you resist spending or help lift your mood.

**SOUL:**

Assess your current money situation. Are there ways to cut back and improve your financial picture? Use these checkpoints mentioned in the chapter to make necessary changes.

___ Do you shop until you drop?

___ Do you spend when you are emotionally upset or need a lift?

___ Are you an impulse buyer who needs to work on self-control?

___ Are you in debt because of credit-card spending?

___ Do you need a financial plan, especially when it comes to saving?

___ Are you living within your means?

___ Do you have an emergency fund saved?

___ Have you planned ahead for predictable expenses?

___ Do you tithe regularly?

**SPIRIT:**

Be faithful in giving.

Meditate on 1 Timothy 6:6-10:

> *Godliness with contentment is great gain. For we brought nothing into the world, and we can take*

*nothing out of it. But if we have food and clothing, we
will be content with that. People who want to get rich
  fall into temptation and a trap and into many foolish and harmful desires that plunge men into ruin and
destruction. For the love of money is a root of all kinds
  of evil. Some people, eager for money, have wandered
from the faith and pierced themselves with many griefs.*

Chapter 10

# Relationship Worries

*We spend precious hours fearing the inevitable.*
*It would be wise to use that time adoring our families,*
*cherishing our friends, and living our lives.*
**—MAYA ANGELOU**

Relationships are satisfying when they work and frustrating when they do not! One thing they can do is provide an immense arena for worry. For example, isn't it easy to worry about whether or not our children are well-adjusted, perform up to their abilities, and are good citizens? If you are a caregiver to elderly parents, worry about finances, good care, and health are high on your list. Then there are the in-laws who may be a challenge, siblings who fight, and neighbors who complain about your yard! It all adds up to restless nights and worse if we are not careful to handle our relationships well.

The main concerns regarding relationships are whether or not they will survive and if they are functional. Since we cannot control what others do, we are open to being hurt or abandoned or feeling rejected. Feelings of vulnerability and powerlessness come into play. And remember, those two ingredients can bring on worry if we let them.

### Vulnerability opens the door to hurt

Brian was excited when he began to date Kelly. She seemed a bit mysterious, which intrigued him. As he spent more time with her, she mentioned her chaotic family. Growing up, nothing in her home life was predictable. Kelly's parents frequently changed jobs, moved around the country, and provided little stability for their children.

When Kelly was 16, her father announced (to the family's shock), that he was leaving. His abandonment left Kelly shaken and unsure of her future. Consequently, she was guarded in her relationship with Brian. Operating out of a fear of being abandoned, she held her cards close to her vest, rarely allowing him to see her true self. This made getting to know her difficult for Brian.

The more he tried to know Kelly, the more she seemed to push him away. Brian did not understand this and worried that she did not like him. Because she was so fearful of rejection, she remained mysterious, a trait he had liked at first but now found frustrating. The relationship tension put a strain on the couple.

Kelly wanted a relationship with Brian, but fear motivated her to stay distant because she worried that he would eventually leave her. Brian, though, had no clue why Kelly remained emotionally distant. They eventually broke off their relationship. This can happen when two people do not work on past issues, do not share their present-day fears openly, or both.

In relationships, we want people to be emotionally accessible and responsive to our needs. As two people get to know each other, two things can happen:

1. One or both can decide to risk being vulnerable. This usually works to strengthen the relationship bond.

2. One or both can decide to be guarded, angry, or withholding. This usually disrupts the bond.

Brian and Kelly were guarded, not vulnerable with each other. Worry over possible hurt blocked intimacy from growing.

### Risk-taking in a relationship

Kelly's failure to communicate her feelings of abandonment created a paralyzing fear. Brian interpreted her emotional distance as a lack of interest in him. The result of this miscommunication was a breakup.

In order for their relationship to grow, Kelly needed to tell Brian why she was hesitant to confide in him or take a chance of being hurt. First, she would need to decide if he could be trusted with her feelings.

In order to do that, she would have to separate her feelings about her father from Brian and decide if Brian was a different type of man than her father. This would require her to take a risk—being willing to become vulnerable.

When someone chooses to be vulnerable in a relationship, hurt can be an outcome. We do not know how another person will react to our deepest thoughts and feelings. This is one reason why relationships are so difficult. Had Kelly decided to be vulnerable with Brian, their relationship could have progressed—or still ended. The outcome would also have depended on how well he handled her feelings. If he was uncomfortable with vulnerable feelings, he might have pushed her away.

On the positive side, when you are vulnerable with someone who can be trusted, the bond grows stronger, and your need to be accepted and loved is fulfilled. Thus, the goal of one type of counseling for couples is to provide a safe haven where they can identify and express their deepest feelings without worry. This kind of therapy is structured to help them create that place of safety so they can work on creating a strong emotional bond.

Unfortunately, many people do not feel safe in their ability to express their deepest feelings in their relationships. When this is the case, anxiety and worry develop. And that is what happened to Kelly. She worried that her relationship with Brian would turn out like her parents' relationship. Consequently, she was not willing to be vulnerable because she was unsure of what Brian would do with her emotions. And her worry made things even worse. She stayed distant. Eventually, what she feared came true.

Brian's lack of understanding and interest in how Kelly's past motivated her current behavior caused him to misinterpret her actions as lack of interest. Because of his own intimacy difficulties, he was not comfortable pushing her for an explanation. In his mind, it was easier to give up on her and move on. He thought she was too much work and wanted to be with someone who was more emotionally accessible.

### Working things through

Karl and Rita had a different outcome regarding their relationship despite their difficulties. Karl was an Iraq war veteran who had witnessed a great deal of death and dying overseas. The trauma of those experiences manifested in post-traumatic stress disorder (PTSD). Intimacy with his wife was difficult after his return. He constantly worried that something bad would happen to his wife and children—so much so that he tried to keep them from leaving the safety of their home.

Rita and Karl had two children and were committed to making their relationship work. As much as Karl hated the idea of therapy, he agreed to go in order to get help with the PTSD that was interfering in his family life. As he recognized how the disorder fed his fears of intimacy and loss, he and Rita created a safe haven in their relationship so he could work through those issues. Rita's participation in the counseling transformed her anger to support and compassion. The couple turned the negative cycle of fighting to a positive one. Karl learned that his worry was based on war trauma and fears of dying. He could conquer that worry by dealing with past traumas and not allowing them to dictate his present. He learned to control his thoughts when a family member left the house and not let worry take charge. Most important, the couple chose to work through relationship problems and developed a strong bond of intimacy.

**Powerlessness**

If you feel like a victim, worry is usually present. Victims feel powerless. When you feel powerless, worry results. Basically, a victim feels like life is totally out of his or her control and gives up. Understanding how to handle feelings of powerlessness in relationships is critical to moving past worry, especially when you take the victim stance.

*What can you control?*

Let me use an extreme example to make a point. A woman who is being beaten by her husband feels powerless. She is a victim of his abuse. Worry is a natural outcome of staying in such a relationship. She may not physically survive another beating. This is real and a constant threat.

Is she completely powerless in this situation? No, she can leave her husband with the help of people trained in domestic violence who know how to keep her safe. Would leaving be hard to do? Yes, because there is always the chance that her abuser would find her or make her life miserable—this is why she needs the help of professionals and shelters. But her worry will never leave if she stays in the situation and remains a victim.

The point here is this—*the only thing we can control is how we respond* to other people. What we do *not* have control over is how they treat us. And this is scary sometimes. Unfair treatment happens. The lack of control we have over other people is frustrating, irritating, and annoying in relationships. But in truth, you have no control over what other people do. Oh, you can influence them, but ultimately another person can behave in ways that make you crazy and, at times, may even be dangerous! Recognizing this type of powerlessness is critical to developing any healthy relationship.

What happens far too often, however, is we act as though we *can* control another person. This sets up worry. Think about it. If you think you have control over someone else's behavior, you constantly worry about how your actions might change that person. For example, the abused wife may think, "If only I never upset my husband, he won't get so angry." This is complete nonsense because not only is it unrealistic (who never upsets another person?), but it also assumes that she is somehow responsible for his abuse. The truth is, he is the only one responsible for it. He must learn to cope better with life and stop. He can get help and change, but not because she has the power to make him do so. He has to be willing to change.

### Making room for change

When we recognize we are powerless to make other people change, this actually empowers us—to react to them in ways that are healthy. So the abused wife needs to see that her husband has an anger problem. A healthy reaction to a man who refuses to stop abuse is to leave him until he accepts responsibility for his problem and gets help. The wrong thing to do is stay and be abused, thinking she can change him.

Now let's apply this idea of powerlessness in a less extreme way. Say you are a husband whose wife constantly criticizes you. You have repeatedly asked her to stop, and you worry that if she continues, resentment will grow. You have told her that her criticism really bothers you and is negatively affecting your relationship. For whatever reason, she does not stop. So what can you do? Keep after her to change? Yes, but nagging does not usually motivate people. Yet this is what people do—work harder at doing the same thing that does not work while trying to change the other person.

When all your nagging and pleading does not work, you feel powerless to make changes. That powerlessness leaves you vulnerable to bad feelings. Then divorce becomes a real worry, because criticism begins the cycle of emotional distance that leads to divorce.

What would happen if instead of focusing on what your wife needed to do, you focused on reacting differently to the criticism? In other words, what if the powerlessness empowered you to make a change? So the next time she criticizes, you walk away and tell her that if she continues, you will choose not to be with her. She does not listen and criticizes you. You walk out of the room. Doing this, you move out of the victim position and take charge of what you can change—your reaction.

The interesting part of changing your reaction is that it changes the negative cycle and eventually (when she sees you mean business) may change your wife. She will no longer see you as powerless. This will impact the relationship. So even though you feel powerless, you are not.

### The other person's response

Now if you make a change in the way you respond, you might worry that your wife will get so angry that she will criticize even more. She might. But instead of worrying about this, hold your ground. Making change means shaking up the current patterns of interaction. If you hold firm, she will eventually change her behavior because you are different. The interaction is not the same because you have changed it. When you behave differently, the other person responds differently.

Here is an example to illustrate this idea. Tom and a church leader had a disagreement. Tom believed the leader was wrong about something that was creating a big problem. He confronted the man. When he did, the leader—who was the pastor—rebuked Tom and told him he was being negative and should stop complaining and grumbling. Tom was not complaining–rather, he was trying to work through a conflict that had caused problems and needed to be resolved. The pastor told Tom that he needed to submit to his authority because he was in charge. (I have seen this happen too many times.) In truth, the leader was trying to intimidate Tom and head off any confrontation.

Tom took issue with the leader's attempt to manipulate the conflict. But Tom worried that he would lose his standing in the church if he challenged the other man. He backed off from resolving the issue but remained anxious about it for months. The relationship between him and the other man was strained. The leader worried that Tom would bring up the issue again, so he reinforced Tom's obligation to be submitted to authority. Tom worried he had done the wrong thing by confronting the leader (he had not) and that he could no longer be effective in the church. There was no trust or dealing with the conflict between the two men. The issue remained unresolved.

Could Tom make the pastor become a less insecure person and confront the problem? No, he had tried to confront him and even enlisted others to help with the confrontation. But the leader had refused to deal with the issue and, in fact, had used his position of power to coerce Tom to drop the conflict.

After several months of worry, Tom tried another approach and took two elders with him to confront the leader. The man still refused to deal with the issue. Finally Tom took the matter to the church board. They had the authority to deal with the leader and did so to Tom's satisfaction.

The point to note is that Tom did not give up even though the pastor tried hard to force him to back down. Tom did not want to leave his church, but he had to address this unresolved conflict. It was eating at him. So he changed his focus from the unfair actions of the leader to what he could do. He could hold on to worry. Or he could operate out of his faith belief—confront the person using the biblical model noted in Matthew 18, and forgive even though the pastor was not asking for forgiveness. Regardless, Tom needed to forgive him. It was God's job (and the board's) to deal with the leader, since Tom could make no progress with him. Tom's choice was to be obedient to what he believed and forgive. This freed him to move forward in his spiritual life and not get stuck in worry. When he stopped doing what did not work (silently worry) and started taking action in a new way (engaging the board), the issue finally was resolved.

When you feel stuck in a relationship, shift your focus away from the other person and to yourself. Carefully think about your behavior and decide if you need to make a change. Changing your reaction will change the "relationship dance" if you do not give in and go back to your old response. Remember, you cannot change another person, but you can change the way you respond to that person, and that changes the relationship dynamic.

## Build trust

Doubt builds in a relationship when people are not honest and not communicating. If you have doubt about a friend, for example, you won't trust her. This is what happened to Vicky. She discovered that her best friend, Ann, was talking behind her back. Ann told mutual friends that Vicky used to party hard when they were in college. In fact, she discussed her drinking habits in great detail with people who barely knew Vicky. Vicky was not proud of her past behavior and did not want other people gossiping about her mistakes. It hurt to know that her best friend talked behind her back.

When she confronted Ann, Ann downplayed the comments and insisted it was not a big deal. But the denial created an open wound of distrust. Vicky knew Ann was not honest with her because several of their mutual friends called Vicky to tell her what Ann had said. She could no longer trust Ann with personal issues. The friendship was strained.

When there is a lack of trust, worry is constantly present. Trust is a key element of any relationship. Without it, worry enters and creates problems.

### Trust increases with openness

Ray struggled with commitment. He dated several women whom he knew would make great partners but always backed out of these relationships when intimacy grew. He worried he would be alone for the rest of his life because he feared commitment. He was an adult child of divorce and did not want to experience the bitter divorce he had witnessed with his mom and dad.

Even though Ray knew his commitment phobia was based on his childhood experience, he did not do anything about it. When Rachel came into his life, things changed. He was totally taken with her but still afraid to commit. Rachel finally gave him an ultimatum—marry me or break up. Ray was worried. This was not a relationship he wanted to lose. After talking to a close friend, he mustered up the courage to go to counseling and work through the pain of his parents' divorce. He knew this was at the root of his fear of commitment. He had to be open about this. Once he did, trust began to build.

It is not always easy to admit that you might be the source of a relationship problem. However, when you are open and willing to work on issues, trust can be built, and there is hope for the relationship.

Worrying whether or not a relationship will survive does you no good. How you react and behave in a relationship influences its survival. That is what you control. When a relationship is stuck, falters, or is unhealthy, change your reaction and see if it changes things. Stop focusing on what the other person needs to do differently. To move forward, action is needed, not worry.

**Be clear about your expectations**

The process of making relationships worry-free includes being clear about what you want and need. Then, stick to your principles (the difficult part). When you clarify your needs but then compromise, this is a setup for worry. For example, if you want to marry a man who is monogamous but then date men who are not, you had better start worrying. Chances are they will not change for you. Too often, men and women are clear about their expectations but compromise their behavior. This is an invitation for worry.

On the other hand, your expectations can be so unrealistic that you never find a committed relationship. Review your expectations and make sure they are realistic. People are not perfect. If you expect to meet someone who qualifies for every item on your wish list, reconsider your expectations. It is good to know what you want in a partner, but do not make your expectations so grand that no one will fit the bill.

Take Tonya, for example. She was determined to hold out for a man who had good character, was attractive, came from a healthy family, and made a six-figure salary. At the age of 35, she began to worry if she would ever find her life partner.

When Tonya and I reviewed her list of expectations, I had her revisit the salary question. Was the six-figure income really a deal breaker? After much soul-searching, she decided it was not. There was a man at her church who was interested in her but made less than $100,000. She had turned him down for several dates, knowing he worked for a nonprofit company, even though she was very attracted to him. When she loosened her expectations without compromising her values, her dating improved. She became hopeful, not worried, about finding a partner.

Some of you may be thinking, "That's fine for Tonya, but *I'm* waiting for my dream person." If you can do that and not be consumed by worry, go for it. But I would advise you to look at your expectations and decide which of them are based on healthy elements of relationships (trust, honesty, integrity, and so on). Sometimes, the things we think we need to make us happy have nothing to do with what works in a relationship.

### In the family: Worry about your children

It seems that parents worry more about their children today than parents did a generation ago. There are a number of reasons for this. The world feels more frightening than days gone by. I grew up in a time when we never locked our doors and we trusted our neighbors. I walked to school with no fear of being kidnapped. No one cyberbullied me because we did not have digital technology. I did not feel pressured to wear designer clothing because advertisers were not in my face 24/7. The list could go on and on. The point is that the rapid pace of change has impacted families in positive and negative ways, thus giving us more to worry about. Parenting requires us to keep current with change so we can help our children. This can be worrisome.

### *The question of independence*

I was thinking about this the other day when I helped my son with a number of college forms. When I applied to college, my parents never helped me with the application. They were great parents but did not worry about the application process. I was expected to figure it out on my own. Whatever happened, happened and was considered part of my growing independence.

This parenting moment made me wonder if we do too much for our kids because we want them to be happy and accomplished. Do we undercut their independence by doing for them? Think about it. Do you worry if they will get the best education, be chosen for the team, find good friends, discover their passion, know their purpose, and live spiritually strong lives? These are all good concerns, but does worry really help them achieve these goals? And are we careful not to care more about the outcome of their actions, and spend more energy trying to make things happen, than they do?

### *Just surviving*

On the other hand, some of you worry if you can make it through the day. With the rise in single parenting, economic stress, and family breakups, your children have to be doing for themselves because you are focused on survival. In these cases, their needs can be overlooked and underserved. So the issue is balance. Regardless of your circumstances, meet the needs of your children without underserving or overserving them. In the process, you must be careful not to let worry get the best of you.

When I begin to wonder how the future will be for my kids, I can feel anxiety start to rise because I have a glimpse of the world they will face. Then I remind myself that I did okay despite life's challenges. I did not have the opportunity to go to the most elite schools. I had no special privilege or economic advantage, but I did have parents who loved each other and did the best they knew how to do. More important, my parents taught me the power of faith. When I am weak, God is strong. He orders my steps. I am not alone in this journey but have the promise of a hope and a future. Faith is where we rest as parents.

Not in the hope that every opportunity will come our child's way, but knowing that our child's life has a plan that will be accomplished when submitted to God.

### Letting them be themselves

Children have so much opportunity in our culture that caring parents do not want to miss even one moment that might bring out talent or lead to something special. But we have to be careful that in our zest for our children's best, we do not confuse our dreams with theirs.

I often listen to the conversations of moms in my daughter's dance classes. You can pick out the ones who have crossed the line. They are so worried about their daughter's dance careers that any little thing sets them off. I know dance is competitive, but I often wonder who is more invested—the mom or the child. As children grow, even talented dancers may not choose dance as a career, or may lose interest, suffer an injury, or simply find a passion elsewhere. The question is, can parents come to terms with this outcome after spending time and money in dance education? Hopefully so!

A challenge in raising children is to know how to guide them in their uniqueness and in following their dreams. Worry can be eliminated when we follow *God's* path for our children, not ours. Along the way, children struggle, but this builds character. We do not want to thwart those necessary struggles. Rest in the promise given to us in Jeremiah 29:11: "'I know the plans I have for you,' declares the LORD, 'plans to prosper you and not to harm you, plans to give you a hope and a future.'"

### Focusing on choices and consequences

You do have control over helping your children understand the consequences of their choices. For example, if your child eats junk food and gains weight, you have a choice. You can worry about the stigma of being overweight, or you can guide your child in making healthy food choices and understanding the consequences of his choices. If your son chooses friends who act out, he needs to understand the trouble that can result and be directed toward better choices. Negative consequences hopefully influence future decisions. Parenting is about guiding children to make good choices in life.

Parenting is exhausting but rewarding when you invest the time and energy to teach your children to choose wisely, problem-solve, and face the consequences of their actions. Our job is not to sit around and worry about their decisions (that is exhausting!), but to guide and teach them. Get involved. Know their friends. Monitor where they go. Investigate their actions. Be available for and open to discussion. Influence their thinking by speaking into situations. Teach them faith and moral living. Understand their hearts. Pray with them and let them know you are on their team. But do not do for them, fail to let them struggle at times, neglect their needs, or fail to teach them personal responsibility and accountability.

When it comes to parenting, you can worry about any number of things, or you can do the best you can and trust God to help you and them along the way.

### WORRY ABOUT YOUR DYSFUNCTIONAL FAMILY

Growing up in a dysfunctional family teaches you dysfunctional behavior patterns. Most of us can identity at least a few things we learned in our families that we would prefer not to pass on to the next or current family. Because no one's family is perfect, you will bring baggage to any relationship.

The important issue is not *if* you have baggage, but how much— and what will you do with it? Worry can be eliminated when people admit to their negative relationship patterns, work on them, and move on with life. The problem is, people are either unaware of how their original families influence them, or they choose not to work on eliminating baggage. Either way, you will become a source of worry to someone else or yourself.

Relationships that are worry-free are not those without drama or problems. They are relationships in which both people agree to keep plugging away at becoming better people. People in worry-free relationships know they have problems, but agree to do something about them. They stop denying their own issues, admit when they are wrong, and make changes along the way. There is a commitment to work through issues, not threaten divorce or operate in denial.

## In the family: worry about Mom and Dad

I am in the stage of life that involves taking care of my elderly parents. My father is 90, and my mom died recently at age 84. Both lived long and productive lives. Aging presents multiple challenges. For many of us who are caretakers, the tendency to worry about elderly parents can keep us up at night. As their health fails and their independence begins to fade, the challenges of providing care while respecting their dignity can be difficult.

Rather than worry, be informed and make plans. It helps to have difficult conversations with your parents as early as possible. I will never forget when my brother and I convinced our parents to make plans regarding their funerals. We did not want to worry about what to do in the midst of our grief when one of them died. So in order to respect their wishes and know what they wanted, we not only had to talk about the funeral, but also visit the funeral home and make arrangements. I thought this would be a morbid experience. Surprisingly, it was not. And the worry we all had about what to do when each of them dies was relieved.

The same is true about caretaking. What plans have been made, if any? Unfortunately, families cannot always meet the needs of elderly parents, and they need a plan of action that takes account of availability of care, cost of care, and logistics. In the world of caretaking, information is power. The more you know about services and legal issues, the less worried you need be. So my advice in this area is to be informed, go to free seminars, do your research, and talk with your parents. Respect them but push them to plan ahead for more difficult days. If you are the elderly parent, do not leave the decisions for your care in the hands of your children. Make plans.

∽

The bottom line with relationships and worry is this. Do what you can to be the best person possible in a relationship. Beyond that, you cannot control other people—and worry does not accomplish anything! Stop worrying and start working on *you*. Problem-solve where you can, set limits and boundaries, and examine your response to a problem relationship. What can you change about the way you react? And stop worrying about what the other person needs to do!

## Worry-Free Exercise

**BODY:**

Focus on your actions and reactions in your relationships. Practice self-soothing and relaxation methods when tension builds. Take a time-out when you need to cool down. Work on communication and problem-solving.

**SOUL:**

Identify one area of your life you can change to be a better person. Make that a goal and watch how that change impacts your relationships. Once you get your eyes off other people and onto your own weaknesses, real change begins to happen.

**SPIRIT:**

Meditate on Psalm 4:4-5:

*Complain if you must, but don't lash out.*
*Keep your mouth shut, and let your heart do the talking.*
*Build your case before God and wait for his verdict* (MSG).

# Chapter 11

# How to Live in the Moment

*If you worry about the future, and dwell
on the past, you can't enjoy the present.*
**—EMILY GIBBONS**

Saying goodbye to worry requires an acceptance of what happens in life, but also a willingness to change. At first, this may sound like a contradiction, but it is not. We can accept what is happening right now in our lives but know, because of our past issues, present circumstances, and future challenges, that change may be required. Here is an everyday example.

### Acceptance with change

Jennifer finds her job rather boring. Consequently, she does not look forward to going to work. She took the job because she was desperate and needed work. Jobs are hard to find right now so she endures the boredom. However, she feels trapped.

Having done her research, Jennifer knows that to change jobs and enter a new field of more interest to her, she must go back to school for more education. She cannot do that until she saves money over the next year.

But Jennifer came to realize she could change her situation by accepting where she is at present. Instead of worrying about her boring job, she decided to approach it differently. Because the job is not challenging, the work is easy. Because it is easy, there is little stress. This affords Jennifer free time to plan career steps, search for a better job, and attend seminars and workshops.

Jennifer felt miserable because all she did was think how much she hated her job. Her new goal was to accept the current situation but plan for future change. When she developed a plan, she was free to enjoy the present. Even though her work was boring, her focus on the positive aspects of the job made a difference in her attitude.

In life, we must be careful not to allow our past issues or future concerns to overwhelm the present. Worry-free people know how to seize the moment, be content, and enjoy the present. This usually requires us to focus on the positives of the moment and remain optimistic. Jennifer had a job, was paying her bills, and was saving for future change. All of this was positive! There were good people in her office, and the work environment was satisfactory. As she accepted what was and stayed optimistic, she was able to enjoy the present. Worrying had not helped her in any way. It had only made her miserable.

Renee's problem differed from Jennifer's. Instead of worrying about the future, Renee would not let go of the past and enjoy the moment. Her past was littered with sexual promiscuity. She felt dirty and shamed for the number of sexual relationships she had had prior to her conversion to Christ. She worried that no man would accept her, that she was damaged goods, and that her past would prevent anyone from loving her in a healthy way.

As she sought godly counsel, she began to understand that once she repented of her past sexual failures, God not only forgave her, but also blotted out her sin. He sees her clean and whole and does not use her past against her. This revelation, backed by Scripture, was life changing, and she was released from worry. Renee recognized that while she still needed to come to terms with the emotional fallout from her past behavior, her clean start with God put worry to rest. Now she could enjoy God and the life He had given her, knowing that she was working on past issues but was no longer a victim of shame.

**When the moment does not look very positive**

But what about those times in life when the present is stressful? How do we accept what seems to be difficult and still believe that God has our back? Yesterday I received an e-mail from a woman who was dealing with this very issue. She was depressed and anxious because her husband of 26 years had left her and was now with another woman. With his new girlfriend in tow, he had stopped by the house to pick up their son. The new couple appeared happy and in love. This devastated the ex-wife. She was struggling with how unfair it all seemed. She, the one trying to take the high road, was depressed and lonely. Her husband, who had had an affair and was now with another woman, appeared to be happy and blessed. She was anxious and miserable. The present moment was painful.

I felt for her. To see your ex with another woman is never easy after a difficult divorce. But my response to her was to urge her to guard her heart. Just because her ex looks happy now does not mean there are no consequences for his actions. Right now, she must be careful to not allow anger and unforgiveness to take hold of her. Her ex-husband appears unwilling to change and acts insensitively toward her. This is a reality she must accept—an unpleasant reality.

One day, this woman's ex will answer to God for the way he treats her, but the only change she can control is in her heart. She cannot allow bitterness to replace her joy or rob her of a contented life. Even though she does not see it, God is working on her behalf because He promises to do so. In the moment, His hand may not be evident. But faith says, trust that God has good things and believe He is with you. Eventually, He will judge each person and justice will be done. In the meantime, we are responsible for our own actions and reactions. It is worth a reminder: We cannot keep bad things from happening.

## Joni's story

I know of no one who demonstrates this delicate balance of acceptance and change better than Joni Eareckson Tada. I had the good fortune to hear her again about a year ago at a national counselors' convention. Each time I hear her speak, I am inspired and humbled. Most of you are familiar with her story.

In 1967, a diving accident left her a quadriplegic and wheelchair-bound. Post-accident, this 17-year-old found herself suicidal desperately trying to come to grips with her faith. Her initial search for answers involved a series of questions many of us ask when in difficult circumstances. How could a loving God allow such tragedy? And when bad things happen, how are we supposed to trust Him? Do we really see negative circumstances as an opportunity for the demonstration of His power? Who is in control here?

Her search for answers led her to the life of Christ. When she contemplated His death on the cross, she concluded that God's will was for Him to die. But how could something that seemed so evil be a part of God's will? Her answer—heaven and hell both participate in the same events on earth.

When Judas betrayed Jesus, when the mob clamored for Jesus' death, when the Roman soldiers tortured Him, and when Pilate sentenced Him to death, hell was at work. Yet Acts 4:28 tells us that these men participated in what God had decided beforehand. God was in the moment.

The triumph of the cross demonstrates that when hell is at work, heaven is also operating. Satan's plan was to destroy Jesus, but God's plan was to use this horrific event to save mankind. In her life's story, Joni points out that God reaches into evil and brings good for us and for His glory. At the cross, history's worst murder became His most glorious moment.

### Seeing God in your moments

The application for our lives is the same: Heaven and hell participate in the same events. And while suffering remains a mystery, it brings glory to God when we refuse to be shipwrecked by it because of our faith. Worry plays a large role in that shipwrecking. An all-wise God often uses the traumas and difficulties of our life to bring about change in us and glorify His name, but worry, fear, and anxiety can sidetrack us from His purposes.

Suffering has a purpose even though there is no goodness in it. God brings goodness out of it although He never thinks suffering is a good thing. His promise is that all things will work together for His plan and purpose in our lives. When He does permit suffering, it changes us. We can become bitter and despairing and conclude He cannot be trusted. Or we can trust, sit back, and watch what He does.

It is in the acceptance of suffering that we begin to get a glimpse of a better day. Change will come. Our bodies will be glorified, our tears removed, and our joy made complete. This acceptance, looking toward eternity, brings peace. An acceptance of what is and the promise of a better tomorrow allow us to live in the moment without worrying about the future. The future is decided—and it turns out well for those who love God!

With our hearts fixed on heaven, we can live worry-free on earth. The choice is ours to accept the moment and allow God to change us. What happens in life is something we cannot control, but who gets the glory is up to us.

When you hear Joni speak, you see that her suffering has brought her an awareness and acceptance of God that most of us have yet to realize. Each time I listen to her deal with a new aspect of pain, I see His grace, and I see a person who trusts in His goodness despite her life circumstances. It is humbling.

Last year, she updated the audience regarding her increasing pain. As I recall, her husband used to turn her twice a night to help her sleep. Lately, he had had to do this five times a night. As she lay in bed each night and begged God to please take away her pain, she again saw a picture of Christ on the cross. She could see His bloodied feet and knew what it meant to take part in His suffering. In her mind, she grabbed those feet, bloodied and bruised for her. To that cross she took her pain and laid it down once again, and repented for complaining.

Her message was that suffering is part of our fallen world, but rather than wallow in it, take it to the feet of Jesus. He handles our distress and brings supernatural peace to the moment. In the end, God wants us to conclude what Job did—that He is good no matter what.

**Give up the illusion of control**

Since a main reason for worry is uncertainty, accepting this reality without becoming anxious is foundational to letting go of worry. It requires giving up the illusion of control.

As we learned early on, anticipating negative events does not affect whether or not they will actually happen. Therefore, we have to mentally embrace an uncertain future, knowing that God is in control and promises to be with us through whatever difficulty we may face.

A recent conversation with an old college friend reminded me of how little control we really have in life. She called to tell me that her husband of 20 years had died unexpectedly. He had recently been to his doctor for an annual physical and had been given a clean bill of health. A few days later he was sitting at the kitchen table, suddenly had trouble breathing, and passed away within minutes. After immediately calling 9-1-1 and administering CPR, my friend knew he was not responding. His death was sudden, traumatic, and totally unexpected. This type of trauma would put most of us in an anxious state.

The shock and denial associated with his death have now worn off. Although the everyday awareness of her loss is beginning to be more real, her attitude and response to her husband's death can only be explained by her active faith. Her acute awareness of life's uncertainty is at an all-time high, but so is her willingness to trust God for today and for the future.

When I spoke to her, she was grieving, but was experiencing a peace that could only come from her intimate walk with God. Her husband had been in full-time ministry, and she was determined that she would live out the message he had preached to so many people over the years. Either God is who He says He is, or He is not.

Everything in her life was changing, but there was an acceptance of what was. Several times, she told us she did not question God. It was a waste of her time and energy. Her marriage had been wonderful, and she was grateful for the time she had had with him and the children they had parented. She did tell God that she preferred to have her husband alive on earth instead of with Him. Life without her husband would not be easy, but with God by her side, she was confident she could deal with this next chapter.

She talked about small things that made her cry and miss him. Through an hour of conversation, it was evident she was operating in reality and was accepting of his death. God's grace was present, and His power was sustaining her through this difficulty. Worry was not a part of her thinking, though it could easily have overtaken her mental state.

I pray for her, but do not worry if she will come through this. Despite the pain and the difficult days that will follow, she is operating in the trust that God has not abandoned her. God's rod and staff are comforting her. She is living out the familiar words of Psalm 23. Her faith is real. Her conclusion? God can be trusted despite her circumstances.

## Live in the moment

To live in the moment requires attending to the moment, a skill many of us ignore. Most of us are so future-driven we do not enjoy the moment. This point was brought home to me during a recent visit with a well-known TV actor. I listened to him speak to an audience of up-and-coming producers, directors, and actors. His dream as an aspiring actor had been to be in a situation comedy one day. For years, he had perfected his acting craft and performed for audiences. Even though he was grateful to have work as an actor, he had been so anxious about the future that he had not been able to enjoy the present. Anxiety gripped him on a daily basis.

As you might guess, he achieved his dream a number of years later. The coveted situation comedy role was his, but the joy he expected at achieving his desire was missing. It was then he realized that all the worry and anxiety over accomplishing the goal kept him from enjoying the ride to the top. When he arrived, he felt rather empty.

The lesson he so poignantly gave the audience was to enjoy every moment, live in the present, and let God take care of your future. Do not get so caught up in what might be that you do not embrace the present and miss out on moments of joy. Of all the things he could have shared about his experiences in Hollywood, this message was on his heart. Pause, enjoy now. Do not worry about tomorrow. God will take care of it.

Right now, what do you feel and what are you thinking? Do you feel tense? Are you thinking about something that could go wrong? Are you so caught up in worrying about the future that you cannot enjoy today? Or are you so anxious about the past that you cannot focus on today? Observe your thoughts and feelings. Worried people usually feel tense or stressed. They do not relax in the moment. Negative thoughts of *what-if* flood their minds.

Focus on the moment and try to accept things just as they are. Do not think about your mistakes, consider what you need to do next, or listen to the voice of self-criticism. Simply be in the moment. Be still. Do as Scripture admonishes. Do not worry about tomorrow. Tomorrow will take care of itself.[1] Listen. Anchor your thoughts in God and accept His love, mercy, and care for you. Rest in those thoughts for a moment.

Whenever I feel worry creeping into my day, I do the above. I stop, focus on the moment, move my attention to God, and bathe in His grace. This small pause helps me refocus, grab anxious thoughts, and take them captive. By reaffirming who God is and how He orders my steps, I can let go of worry.

### JUST BREATHE AND RELAX

In order to change your worried state, focus first on your body. Right now, take a few deep breaths. Deep breathing relaxes the body. Here is how you do it:

1. Place your hand on your abdomen right beneath your rib cage.

2. Inhale slowly and deeply through your nose. If you are breathing deeply, your hand should rise on your stomach.

3. Pause a moment.

4. Now exhale slowly through your nose and mouth. As you exhale, allow your body to relax.

5. Do this ten times and your body should release tension and relax.

If you cannot relax with breathing alone, practice muscle relaxation as described in chapter 4. To enjoy the moment, it is important to attend to body tension and try to relax. Taking deep breaths and practicing muscle relaxation are two easy ways to calm physical tension. Next, attend to your thoughts. They too must be calmed and captured as we discussed in chapter 6.

## Quiet your mind through prayer and meditation

Scripture admonishes us to meditate day and night on God's Word. It brings physical, emotional, and spiritual healing and peace to our minds. When thoughts are racing in my head and I cannot sleep, I will often focus on a portion of Scripture or on the name of Jesus. Meditation allows us to just be in the moment with God. It stops everything else and brings attention to the here and now. It makes us aware of His presence.

Christian meditation is distinctly different from Eastern forms of meditation, which are so popular today. You have probably heard the term *mindfulness*. This usually refers to having a present-moment orientation. It is used in mental health to deal with pain and stress.

In Eastern meditation, one empties the mind and detaches from all thoughts. Thoughts are not judged. Christian meditation is distinctly different. The New Testament refers to the mind as in need of constant renewal.[2] Its tendency is to wander away from the thoughts of Christ.

In Christian theology, our thoughts are important and will be judged, as Jesus noted in Matthew 5:28. And the apostle Paul reminds us that nothing good lives in us.[3] In other words, our unenlightened minds are not capable of enlightenment on their own. And while mindfulness practices that do not include God may relieve stress, they cannot bring wholeness to a person because they do not bring life to the spirit. True *rest* comes from the person of Christ,[4] and it cannot be imitated through self-effort.

Eastern meditation aims to awaken inner strengths and wisdom apart from God.[5] The Bible says wisdom apart from Him is foolishness and futile. Wisdom, for the believer, is knowledge of His will and of Him.[6] Wisdom is not a mystery reserved for a select few but is open to anyone who seeks God. It does not come by transcendence of the mind but is given by Him.

Christian meditation focuses on the person of God. Psalm 1:2 tells us that the blessed man meditates on God's laws day and night. The psalmist also prayed that the meditations of his heart would be acceptable to God, implying not only a personal relationship, but also judgment of right and wrong. The Christian mind is to be filled with thoughts of God, who indwells our spirit. The divine Christ inhabits our spirit.

For Christians, mindfulness is an active process between God and man. He is mindful of us,[7] and we are to put on the mind of Christ. To do so, we meditate on who God is and listen to Him in prayer. Daily, we renew our mind by the power of the Holy Spirit working in us; we love God with all our mind; and we implant His laws into our minds.[8] Meditation is a way to connect with Him, to be with Him, to listen for His voice, and to align our thinking to His. This creates greater intimacy, not detachment.

"Cease striving and know that I am God" is our biblical instruction.[9] Striving only brings anxiety. When we know who God is, we can rest. And the prescription for peace is provided in Philippians 4:5-9—pray, give thanks, let our requests be known to God, and meditate on things that are true, noble, right, pure, lovely, and admirable. The result of this spiritual practice is God's peace (verse 7).

When you feel anxious, meditate on the good things of God. Practice His presence. Worry cannot coexist with God's presence.

## Worry-Free Exercise

**BODY:**

> Practice being in the moment. Focus your attention on your body. Look for signs of tension. Now, relax by taking deep breaths as described above.

**SOUL:**

> 1. Again, focus on the moment. What thoughts are running through your head?
>
> 2. If they are worried thoughts, take them captive and bring them to Christ.

**SPIRIT:**

> Renew your mind with the promises of God and believe that He is working all things for your good. Trust Him and ask Him to help your unbelief. In your distress, He hears you. Thank Him for that truth. Cease striving and know that He is God. Meditate on Philippians 4:6-7:

*Do not be anxious about anything,*
*but in everything, by prayer and petition,*
*with thanksgiving, present your requests to God.*
*And the peace of God, which transcends all understand-*
*ing, will guard your hearts and your minds in Christ Jesus.*

Chapter 12

# Practical Help to Send Worry Packing

*You'll break the worry habit the day you decide you can
meet and master the worst that can happen to you.*

**—ARNOLD GLASOW**

Behind worry is a belief that everything that happens is beyond our control. This is true in many cases, but the worrier goes even further with this belief. Not only is everything out of our control, but also no one is controlling *anything*. There is no God working on our behalf, seeing the big plan or orchestrating our lives. Even when we remember He is present, worriers act as if He is not. Worriers forget about Him, reduce Him to a human level, or do not invite Him into their everyday lives.

Unbelief and lack of awareness do not change the reality that God is present. But they do establish worry. Think about it. To worry means you believe you have no help with and little control over your life. Whatever you do on your own may or may not work out—there's no way of knowing. If I truly believed this, I would be worried all the time! And that is the problem. Too often I forget how big God is, how involved He is in my life, and that He is present. Basically, when I worry, I ignore Him.

When we fully understand who God is and how He relates to us, worry has no place in our lives. Remember, this does not mean that we never suffer or that bad things do not happen. Rather it means that God is always with us, ready to help us through difficulty. We are not alone. With Him in our lives, the promise is that our negative experiences will be used for good and make us stronger. He will get us though whatever we face.

## Distorted views of God

But so many of us operate with misconceptions about God. We misunderstand this all-powerful being and often blame Him for bad things He does not do. A crucial reason for this relates to our experiences with our parents.

### God as a father

We grow up in a family. Our ideas about God are influenced by our experiences of being parented. Our parents serve as prototypes for God, and how they treat us often shapes and forms our opinions of Him and other authority figures. We then transfer our ideas about our parents to God the Father. That transfer is often not based on the reality of who God is, but on our experiences.

So, for example, if our father was authoritarian, we tend to think God is authoritarian. If Dad let us down by not following through on his promises, we think God will do the same. If Mom criticized us often, we think God is critical of us as well. If Dad never corrected us when we did wrong, it is easy to think God does not really care that much about our sin. If your parents expected you to perform to get their approval, maybe you think the same is true about God—you have to perform well for Him to approve of you. The truth is, nothing you do makes you more acceptable to Him. He already accepts you— flaws, failure, and all.

A distorted view of God based on our parenting experiences is often behind thoughts of worry. Distortions lead us to think He cannot be trusted. As we learned in a previous chapter, if He cannot be trusted, then we *should* worry. Without Him and a grand plan, life would be random, based on luck, purposeless—a truly worrisome worldview.

### Evaluating our parents' influence

In order to know how much our ideas about God are influenced by the parenting we had, try this easy exercise. Make three columns on a piece of paper. Label one column *God the Father,* another, *Father,* and a third column, *Mother.* Under the column *God the Father,* list several characteristics of God found in the Bible. Then go to the second and third columns and check off whether or not that characteristic was true of your father and mother. After you finish, compare the differences. This should help you identify where possible distortions concerning God may be.

The example below is based on the responses of a person whose father was not dependable and rarely showed love. As he listed characteristics of God, he was able to see the contrast with his own parents. This exercise helped him rethink his views. He realized that the way he thought about God was greatly influenced by the parenting he received when growing up.

| God the Father | Father | Mother |
|---|---|---|
| 1. Nothing separates me from His love (Romans 8:35-39) | No | Yes |
| 2. He will carry me all the days of my life (Deuteronomy 1:31; Isaiah 46:3-4) | No | No |
| 3. He cherishes and honors me (Isaiah 43:4) | No | No |
| 4. He takes delight in me (Psalm 149:4) | No | No |
| 5. He lavishes me with grace (Ephesians 1:7-8) | No | No |
| 6. He does not remember my sins and wickedness (Hebrews 8:12) | No | Yes |
| 7. He is trustworthy (Psalm 9:10; 33:20-22) | No | Yes |
| 8. He keeps all His promises to me (Joshua 21:43-45) | No | No |
| 9. He wants only the highest good for me (Psalm 31:19) | Yes | Yes |
| 10. He will never lie to me (Titus 1:2) | No | Yes |

On the positive side, if we had or have parents who show godly characteristics, it is easier for us to accept God's love and grace because we see this lived out in our family. A mom who comforts her child when she is hurt helps her daughter see how God can comfort her in difficult times. A dad who unconditionally loves his son helps the son know the unconditional love of God. A dad who gives good things to his daughter helps her accept the good things God has for her. The good we experience in our family helps us accept the goodness of God.

Now look for the positive similarities between the characteristics of your earthly parents and God. In most cases, those exist as well.

The work each of us has to do is to sort through our ideas about God and determine how many are based on our experiences with earthly parents or caretakers rather than on what God's Word says about Him. Did our parents help or hinder us in understanding how to think about Him? Since He is the only perfect parent, chances are we have transferred a few wrong ideas about Him from our parents. The correction is to know the truth and separate it from our parenting experiences.

It is also easy to have a false picture of God if you have been wounded by someone, if you do not know Scripture well, or if you have been taught things about God that are simply not true.

The good news is that when we understand who God really is, none of us are victims. Despite our positive or negative relationships with parents or other life experiences, we can intimately know God by His presence in our lives and by His Word. The truth of who God is corrects the distortions we may have learned in our families, moving us out of the victim role.

### Nonscriptural input can form a wrong view

Some of you had no religious training growing up and developed your own ideas about God based on experiences, the media, or people you knew. Here is an example. When counseling two teenagers who said they were Christians but were sexually active with each other, I asked them how they justified this behavior. They answered, "There is

a love chapter in the Bible, 1 Corinthians 13. It says if you love someone, you could have sex with them."

Boy, were they surprised when we actually looked up the chapter and they could not find what they believed to be true. They were
simply ignorant of what the Bible said—they had believed a few of
their friends who had no idea what they were talking about. When they
discovered that premarital sex was not acceptable, they thought God
would throw them out of Christianity. I had to show them scripturally
that God did not operate that way. His grace and mercy has brought
forgiveness, which we understand when repentance is made. But His
Word is to be a standard by which to live our lives. As with the woman
caught in adultery, Jesus does not condemn us when we sin and then
repent, but He tells us to sin no more.

### Bad theology also distorts who we think God is

Sometimes we develop a false picture of God because we are taught
bad theology. When my son was elementary-school age, he bounded
out of Sunday school one day and said he gave a dollar in the offering.
At the time, he was learning about tithing. But the reason he gave the
money was based on false teaching from the Sunday school teacher.
She had told our son that if he put the dollar in the offering, he would
get three or four dollars back. No scripture supports this notion. Scripture tells us we will be blessed by tithing, but not that the blessing is a
threefold increase in money! If we had not corrected this bad theology,
our son would have been disappointed in God and believed that God
does not do what He says. Bad teaching is prevalent in churches and
in media so you have to test everything by Scripture. And bad teaching can lead to beliefs about God that are not true.

### Emotional wounding distorts our views of God

Finally, when we are emotionally, relationally, or spiritually wounded,
false notions about God can be implanted in our minds. For instance,
when my brother died, the hurt made me vulnerable to believing the lie
that God could not be trusted. I did not want to confront the truth that
He does not stop all bad things from happening. That was too painful! It

was easier for me to be angry with Him. The lie "God cannot be trusted" was implanted in my thinking at the time of my brother's death and grew over the years, causing worry and doubt.

Or think of the woman whose pain of infertility leads her to conclude that God does not care about her; the former addict who believes he is too damaged to be used by God; the man beaten as a child who believes he is not good enough for God; and the perfectionist who thinks she must prove herself worthy to Him.

At the time of any emotional wounding, a lie is easily implanted in our mind. If we do not know the truth about God or if we blame Him for our hurt, then doubt about His character begins to develop. Therefore, we must be careful not to allow those negative thoughts to be implanted when we are wounded or hurt. The way to avoid this is to know God's character and develop a personal relationship with Him. As we study His Word and continue to grow in our understanding of His true character, we are less likely to believe false thoughts when they pass through our minds or when we are taught them.

Again, correct thinking does not guarantee that nothing bad will ever happen or that our lives will be stress free. A friend of mine jokes that when he became a Christian, he was told by the person who introduced him to Christ that he would never have any problems and life would be happy. What a ridiculous idea—one not based on the whole counsel of God. Bad theology!

The truth is, we live in a fallen world, but God is always with us and sees us through difficult times. Without this reassurance, there would be no hope. Life would be random and meaningless, and worry would be about our only option.

### Helpful ways to tolerate distress

God does not abandon us when life gets tough. We are never alone. "The LORD himself goes before you and will be with you; he will never leave you nor forsake you. Do not be afraid; do not be discouraged."[1] Knowing this and knowing that God promises to work all things for our good helps us tolerate distress and gives perspective so the distress does not overwhelm us. We may *feel* abandoned and alone, but that is not reality.

Take a woman who is battling cancer. The chemotherapy is nauseating, the treatments physically exhausting, and the outcome uncertain, but God promises to be by her side through it all. Despite the negative facts you know and what you experience, you are promised God's presence and help. This is comforting. A worried person forgets this and feels as if she must handle life alone.

This lesson was brought home as I watched a television show the other night. In the drama, one of the main characters was battling cancer. She claimed no spiritual life. The fight was full of angst, hopelessness, and depression. Regularly she commented on how random it all was—some people get better, others do not. She worried every day if she would live or die.

What struck me watching this show was the character's complete lack of hope and her resignation to random fate. It was depressing to watch! However, when you include God in the reality of cancer, hope is present, comfort is felt, and His presence brings peace to the moment.

One way to include God and tolerate distress is to think about the thing that causes you distress. As you think of it, practice relaxing your body. As you relax your physical body, take any negative thought and line it up with a godly thought. Imagine God working behind the scenes and stay relaxed.

### Healthy distraction

Learning to tolerate distress may take practice. Most of us are not good at facing the reality of pain and suffering without becoming worried. There is a fine line between awareness of problems (acceptance) and dwelling on them (worry).

When it feels like worry is overtaking you, get your mind off your problems and on to someone else. This is an age-old strategy for feeling better and tolerating distress. Instead of worrying, write someone a letter of thanks, call a friend and offer to run an errand or babysit her child, work at the food bank and compare your situation to someone less fortunate. Someone somewhere is going through a problem bigger than yours. Sometimes this perspective helps us focus less on our personal situation. I am not suggesting we live in denial of our problems, but rather that we put our problems in perspective by becoming other-focused.

As long as the distraction does not include numbing ourselves through addiction or doing something destructive, distraction is a useful tool to get our minds off our problems and on to better things. It is not an escape of reality or pain, but an opportunity to refocus.

And keep in mind that distracting activities are different from attempts to distract our thoughts. We have learned that thought suppression or distracting our minds does not work—but healthy forms of distracting activities give us relief and a new focus. For example, a person cannot problem-solve away cancer but she can stay active in her friendships, read a hopeful story, and talk to a friend in need. Using distraction to cope with reality helps us tolerate distress. It gets our mind off worries and on to other people and other things. Healthy distraction gives worry a time-out.

### Improve the moment

Another strategy we can use to tolerate distress is to "improve the moment." When you feel anxious or worried, imagine a place where you feel safe or secure (for example, in the loving arms of God), pray, try to relax, and focus on getting through this one moment. Encourage yourself that "this too will pass" and that it may be used to bring help to someone in the future or to bring glory to God.

Furthermore, change the focus of your distress. Instead of thinking, "Why me...why is this happening now?" accept the distress as part of the human experience. Like Job, you may never receive the answer to the "Why me?" question. Remember that faith in action is believing what we do not see or understand. Some questions are not answered on this side of eternity. The "why me?" focus rarely takes us anywhere but despair.

### Take one crisis at a time

Therapist Marsha Linehan has a helpful saying: "Focus on one crisis at a time." This is the modern way to say, "Hey, Rome wasn't built in a day!" Most of us have stress in our lives and problems that have yet to be solved, but we cannot tackle everything at once and keep our sanity. Linehan reminds us that we should focus on the issue at hand rather than taking on multiple problems at a time. This fits with the teachings of Jesus—do not worry about tomorrow; it will take care of itself. The expectation that we need to fix every problem or to make every bad thing go away quickly contributes to worry.

### Make a pros-and-cons list

If you worry about decisions you make, write up a list of pros and cons to help you feel better about your decision. When you review the list, it should reinforce why you decided what you did. Such a list is a visual way to help you make decisions and not worry about making a wrong decision. You might make a wrong decision, but at least you will know why you did—the list records your thinking.

Dawn used a pros-and-cons list to help her stop worrying about how to help her aging parents. Guilt was getting the best of her because she lived a thousand miles away from them. To put her worry to bed, she developed a list to analyze the idea of moving closer to her parents' home. When she finished the list, she then assigned a weight or priority to each item. On a scale from one to five, in which one was of low importance and five was most important, she rated each item. For example, giving up her job was on the cons side and rated a five on her scale. When she finished and reviewed her list, many of the cons outweighed the pros. This process helped her be content with her decision to stay where she was.

∽

There are many practical ways to let go of worry. Each one involves changing our beliefs, thoughts, and behavior in some way. If these ways help us be confident that no problem is too big to handle because of God's involvement in our lives, we can face tomorrow without worry. We can also behave in ways that break the habit of worry and keep us focused on the moment.

## Worry-Free Exercise

**BODY:**

Learn to tolerate stress by using relaxation, a pros-and-cons list, healthy distraction, living in the moment, and dealing with one crisis at a time.

**SOUL:**

Take each of the practical helps offered in this chapter and apply them to an area of worry in your life. In the process, be aware of thoughts that contribute to worry.

**SPIRIT:**

Think about the role hurts and wounds play in making you vulnerable to lies about God. Now take those thoughts and line them up according to what you know about Him. Dig deep in the Bible and learn as much as you can about His character. Count on His character when circumstances are uncertain or difficult.

Meditate on John 14:6 and Jesus' words:

*I am the way and the truth and the life.*

# Chapter 13

# The Secret to Contentment

*I have learned the secret of being content in any and every
situation, whether well fed or hungry, whether living in plenty or
in want. I can do all this through him who gives me strength.*
**—THE APOSTLE PAUL**

Is it one of your life goals to be content? If so, given the culture in which we live, you may find it difficult to reach that goal. Daily, we are bombarded by media messages to never be satisfied with what we have. To be happy, we are told we need more stuff, more power, more money, and more fame. In a word, more is better. We are sold this path to contentment, and apparently we are buying it.

We only have to look at the high rate of consumer debt. People are not content to live within their means. We need bigger houses, more expensive cars, designer clothes, expensive toys, and the latest technology. Get it now. Pay later. You deserve the biggest and the best regardless of what you can afford.

Advertisers convince us that we cannot possibly be happy until we buy their products. They thrive on our discontent. That restless longing for more sells products and motivates us to buy. We must have the latest and newest of whatever in order to preserve our image and keep up with those around us. To be without threatens our self-worth.

A few years ago, I was watching a television commercial depicting a broken relationship between a man and a woman. The woman was very sad, but she brightened up when she saw a new sweater. The tagline of the commercial was, "The relationship might not last, but the sweater will be there forever!" I laughed. Trade a sweater for a man because one brings continued happiness?

### Discontent is everywhere

In our quest for more and better, we are on the move. We look for better jobs and places to live. Job and career changes are often based on where we can find a better lifestyle, cost of living, and opportunities for advancement.

Add to this our discontent in marriage. Divorce rates remain high, and more and more people are cohabitating because of fear of divorce. When a relationship does not satisfy our deepest longings, we look around and think someone else will fill that emptiness or meet that need. Dissatisfaction also leads to clamoring for our rights and for fair treatment. Getting fair treatment and an improved partner are supposed to bring us happiness and put a stop to discontent. But they do not, because discontent in not rooted in the failure of someone else to make us happy or the failure to keep up with trends or find the perfect mate.

Even church organizations experience ongoing discontent. Small churches want to grow bigger, and big churches struggle to meet the intimacy needs of their people. Churchgoers are discontented with their pastors, their boards, the worship style, or their youth leaders. Leaders hear a constant litany of complaints. You would think the purpose of church is to entertain its members. (I am guilty of this thinking myself!) It is easy to allow the culture of discontent to enter our thinking in all areas of our lives. But when we think like this, we become customers of the church, not worshippers.

We are also a culture of constant change. Whether it is in the world of technology, fashion, design, manufacturing...it doesn't matter. We have to keep current. And current means keeping up with trends. From curvy Marilyn Monroe, to sticklike Twiggy, to tall and busty Cindy Crawford, to emaciated-looking Kate Moss, to breast implants for teens, changing images of beauty create ongoing angst in women. We worry that we do not measure up to cultural prescriptions for beauty. We covet outward beauty and youth.

A few years ago, when I wrote a book on body dissatisfaction titled

*Making Peace with Your Thighs*, I was hoping our culture would rethink its fixation on body discontent. Unfortunately, nothing much has changed in the larger culture. We seem headed down the same path of creating more discontent in order to sell more products and services.

Discontent breeds worry. The constant thoughts of "Can I keep up?" "Will I be able to pay for my wants?" "Will it ever be enough?" "Will all these things make me happy?" "If I were married to a different person, would I be happy?" feed discontentment and can eventually lead to sin. Consider Adam and Eve's desire to be like God, Cain's jealousy of his brother, King David's passion for another man's wife, Satan's lust to be worshipped, Judas selling out Jesus for money, Herod's wish to be the one and only king people served. Over time, a growing discontent led to sin in all these examples.

## Contentment in the midst of difficulty

Imagine losing your freedom for what you believe. You are imprisoned and will be executed for your faith. The ruling dictator has already murdered your friend. The night before your execution, you are bound with chains and forced to sleep between two soldiers and the keeper of the door. Would you sleep soundly?

The apostle Peter did. He slept so soundly that the angel of the Lord had to shine an intense light in the prison and hit him on his side to wake him up. Now that is an amazing story! About to be executed, Peter did not spend his last night fretting and worrying. He knew the church was praying for him, but he did *not* know he would walk out of prison that night under miraculous circumstances. He trusted God and His plan for his life, or he would have been a worried wreck! Instead, his mind was kept in perfect peace because it was fixed on God.

### *The apostle Paul and contentment*

Another man sat under house arrest because of corrupt officials who had made false charges against him. He knew all too well what might be ahead of him. He had endured afflictions and suffered numerous hardships. He had been beaten and imprisoned, stoned and threatened with death, shipwrecked three times, experienced sleeplessness and hunger, and endangered by robbers, rivers, seas, his Jewish countrymen, Gentiles, wildernesses, and false brothers.

During this house arrest, he wrote a letter to people who had treated him kindly, the Philippians. The apostle Paul was isolated in that prison cell, unable to preach and physically minister to the church though he was free to write letters and receive visitors and gifts.

Paul knew it had been ten years since the Philippians had heard of his need and sent gifts. But a messenger was sent from Philippi with a gift for him. When the gift arrived, Paul rejoiced in the generosity of the church. He did not complain that it had been ten years since he heard from them. Instead, he gave the church the benefit of the doubt, believing that they simply had not had the opportunity to help him until now.

Scripture tells us that Paul's gratitude for the gift was not based on need. He believed God was taking care of him, and he was satisfied with little even though his needs were great. His patient confidence was founded on God's sovereignty and timing. He knew God would act on his behalf. He placed his life confidently in the Lord's hand.

Paul's experiences through all his trials had taught him that the times and seasons are controlled by God. He believed that God ordered everything for His purposes and was working all things for his good. After thanking the church at Philippi for sending a gift, Paul speaks to the subject of contentment. The secret is revealed in the Philippian letter.

### Christian self-sufficiency

The word translated *content* is the Greek word *autarkes*, meaning to be self-sufficient or independent. Self-sufficiency was considered a virtue in Greek culture and was a common term during biblical times. However, the biblical idea of self-sufficiency differed from that of Greek culture and the Stoic philosophers of the day. The Stoics believed that contentment was reached by being resigned to one's situation. It was a term that referred to total indifference, a sort of ancient version of "whatever" or "I do not care."

Paul's discussion of contentment in Philippians 4 had nothing to do with Stoic indifference. His contentment was rooted in his faith. The deep joy he felt while in jail came through his relationship with God and His goodness in all that happened. Paul's union with Christ, God in Him and with Him, was the secret to being content.

Paul could rejoice in trials because of the fruit they bore and the strength and courage that resulted, not because he had some twisted need to suffer. His words to us regarding being content in any situation are backed up by his own difficult and glorious experiences in life. God strengthened him to persevere during difficulty and thrive during abundance. He came to understand that contentment was learned through his relationship with God, not through his circumstances. Paul never complained that he was a victim of circumstances. He did not worry because he knew God would supply all his needs. That is why he tells us that he could be content with much or little—a striking contrast to our present-day thinking.

## Contentment is learned

Contentment is not something we are given. It does not come because we achieve or accumulate enough things. It is also not a natural state. Rather, contentment must be cultivated. It must be learned. To be content means to be satisfied and at ease with your situation.

This does not imply that you cannot improve yourself or seek to do better. Contentment is not complacency. But when we work to better our circumstances, we must look carefully at the motive behind those actions. Are we motivated out of increasing discontent or extreme worry? God wants us to grow but also be content with the life He has given us for this moment. When content, we are free from greed and slavery to things.

Contentment is in the mind. It is believing that He causes things to work out for our good. He is in control, and we do not need to worry. It is interesting that worry and complaining do not need to be taught. But learning to acquiesce to God and His plans for our lives must be practiced. Eyes that are focused on God prevent us from being thrown around by life's circumstances. Worry cannot take hold.

Paul is a powerful example of someone who did not grumble or complain, panic or worry in the worst of circumstances. He challenges us to not lose perspective when times are tough, to not distrust God, and to patiently submit to His ways. Hope is always present. It was God Himself who brought a quiet calm to Paul's faith. The apostle lived independent of everything and dependent on God. He rejoiced in all circumstances. What a challenge!

### Enjoying dependence

The psalmist David said in Psalm 23, "The LORD is my shepherd, I lack nothing." Do we believe this? If we do, we have no reason to worry.

Often, we have to learn to trust the Lord as our shepherd. The Lord led the children of Israel into the desert so they would learn to trust *Him* and not rely on themselves or the people of any other nation. He sometimes leads us into a wilderness to do the same.

This lesson of complete dependence is a difficult one for people trained in self-sufficiency. It was a lesson I learned through the seven-year struggle I had with infertility. For the first time in my life, I could not make my body do what I thought it was supposed to do—get pregnant. The endless cycles of trying, the painful treatments, and the nights of tears and despair overwhelmed me.

Because nothing I did made a difference, God was the only one who could help me. Sadly, I *ended* my struggle with this conviction, rather than beginning with it. But by His grace I learned I could do nothing apart from Him. I needed His daily presence to keep my sanity, endure the treatment and disappointment, and cope with friends who were having babies.

Daily, my mind had to be renewed with His truth. The truth that He would not abandon, punish, or reject me had to be foremost in my mind to defeat discouragement. As I submitted to His plan for my life concerning children, I had to lay mine down. Concluding that His ways were better than mine, through a long process of surrender I gave in to Him. *Your will, not mine.*

I was raised to be independent and get things done. I can be quite stubborn. But God has a way of reminding us we are not in control and desperately need Him. For me, infertility brought me to that place of complete dependency.

∽

To learn the secret of contentment, we must get our eyes off worry and on to God. He sees our need and is ready, willing, and able to meet it. Since He is in us, He never leaves during difficult times. His spiritual army surrounds us, and His strength is the source of our contentment. As the apostle Paul said, do not be anxious about anything, but in all things be grateful and give thanks. In prayer, present your needs to God. Thank Him for what He will do. And His peace will fill your heart.

When you are tempted to worry, get your eyes off the circumstances and on to God. Think on things that are true, noble, right, pure, lovely, admirable, excellent, and praiseworthy. It will keep you from being shaken and bring the peace you need for that moment. God is with you. Accept His peace. Rest in Him.

## Worry-Free Exercise

**BODY:**

Look around you. What are you grateful for that you can visibly see in your life? Give thanks.

**SOUL:**

1. Do you lack contentment because you have put your trust in things or people that will not deliver true peace?

2. Do you lack contentment because you have bought the lies of our culture in regard to power, fame, materialism, and appearance?

3. If either of the above is the case, turn from a dependence on other people and things.

**SPIRIT:**

Meditate on Psalm 28:7 and give thanks.

> *The LORD is my strength and my shield;*
> *my heart trusts in him, and I am helped.*
> *My heart leaps for joy and I will*
> *give thanks to him in song.*

Chapter 14

# Cultivate a Worry-Free Life

*Do not worry about tomorrow, for tomorrow will worry
about itself. Each day has enough trouble of its own.*
—JESUS CHRIST

As we learned in the last chapter, a worry-free life is cultivated. It does not just happen because "Life is good," as the slogan says. Life is good but also has its moments. Troubling times will come our way. Jesus assures us of this in the book of John when He says, "In this world you will have trouble."[1] Taken alone, this prediction of suffering and difficult times could easily cause us to worry. But Jesus does not stop there and leave us to worry or to despair. He concludes with these powerful words, "But take heart! I have overcome the world." The battle has been won. Death could not hold Him, and He lives in the power of the resurrection. Because of this, we say goodbye to worry and receive God's peace. Jesus' comforting words to us are, "Do not let your hearts be troubled."[2]

It is only possible to live out Jesus' words because He empowers us, through His Spirit living in us, to overcome worry. Time and experience will teach us to walk in confidence no matter what our circumstances.

## Living in God-confidence

The children of Israel had to learn to walk in confidence in God when they were trapped by Pharaoh's army. After pleading with Pharaoh to let God's people go, Moses finally got the green light.

But as they left Egypt, a surprising thing happened. God ordained that Pharaoh's army would pursue His people. You might have trouble with that fact. Numerous times in the Bible, God uses the wickedness of others to accomplish His purposes. Scripture tells us that Pharaoh's anger burned after he allowed Moses and the people to leave. Yes, he had finally acceded to Moses' pleas to let them go, but he changed his mind after the fact. So Pharaoh dispatched his army to pursue the Israelites.

The pursuit came to a crisis point when the people reached the Red Sea. In the natural, the situation looked hopeless. The people were stuck. The sea was too big and deep to cross. Pharaoh's army was in hot pursuit and catching up to kill them. But nothing is too difficult for God. God miraculously parted the sea to allow His children to pass, and then drowned the enemy. Time and again, the message to the Israelites was that if God was for them, they were not to worry. He often told them He would bring victory.

I confess I must remind myself that God brings the victory. Most likely, I would have been one of those Israelites who panicked. It is easy to forget to put on spiritual glasses when circumstances look troubling. Too often, I view situations with my human eyes. I see the large deep sea with no way to cross and fail to trust God to make a way.

The story of the prophet Elisha in 2 Kings 6 is a wonderful reminder that God brings victory and we are not to fear. The king of Syria had declared war on Israel. His plan was to attack, but his intel was that the Israelite army had been warned of his attack. The king then asked his servants how his plan had been revealed. They reported that the prophet Elisha seemed to know the secret plans. So the Syrian king ordered his servant to find and capture Elisha. When the prophet's location was determined, the king sent a great army to surround and besiege the city where Elisha was staying.

The next morning Elisha and his servant arose and saw the Syrians positioned to capture them. The servant panicked, seeing no way of escape.

But the prophet saw what his servant did not—a great army of the Lord full of horses and chariots of fire, surrounding and protecting Elisha, whose spiritual eyes were open. The prophet prayed for his servant's eyes to also be opened to the unseen spiritual realm. Then he prayed for the Syrians to be struck with blindness. God answered his prayer, and Elisha led the blinded army directly to the king of Israel. As the enemy soldiers stood in front of the king, God opened their eyes, and they realized they were captured. Elisha told the king not to kill them but to feed them. He prepared a feast for his enemies and sent them away.

This incredible move of God was enough to stop the raids and keep the Syrians out of the land. Talk about a fear factor! God allowed them to see that when you mess with one of His, there is a spiritual army with which to contend. Once we are aware of God's power, power that is greater than that of our enemy, we are not to fear. The victory is ours!

### A life with God

As I have mentioned several times, living a life of peace and contentment requires an acceptance of life's uncertainties. There are things beyond our control that no amount of worrying will ever change. And there is always a certain amount of risk with any action we take. The path to acceptance of this uncertainty is a life with God. Since nothing happens out of God's awareness, He knows what we face and will not leave us to face it alone. His constant presence reassures us that we can embrace an uncertain future.

That said, we must not be passive in placing our confidence in God. The life of faith is active and requires partnering with Him in all that we do. Peace and rest come when we submit our lives to Him and actively walk out our faith. Along the way, we build our skills of problem-solving, seek wisdom, ask for help, practice self-care, walk in obedience, and live a centered life. The rest of this chapter will focus on various aspects of cultivating such a worry-free life.

### Believe that worry is useless

By now, I hope you are convinced of the power of your thoughts in regard to worry. Beliefs about worry directly influence if and how much we worry. The more we believe worry has a place in our lives, is useful, or provides us benefits, the more we will worry. Until we truly believe that worry is useless, that any positive gains are short-lived, and that it is ultimately damaging, it will be difficult to give up. In order to live a worry-free life, re-examine your beliefs about worry. At this point in the book, where do you stand when it comes to hanging on to worry as helpful? To let go of worry, refuse to think it is beneficial. A life of peace cannot esteem worry in any way.

**Do not overinvest in an outcome**

A life of peace and calm also requires letting go of the outcome of situations. When we desperately want something to turn out a specific way, worry usually accompanies the waiting.

*Trusting God in the process*

This was brought to my awareness in the past month. Our church was in a position to purchase another church building at auction. Due to unforeseen circumstances, a state-of-the art building was for sale at a ridiculously low price. It was basically ready for move-in and appeared to be a beautiful provision for our need of more space. Acquiring it would answer many of our space and growth problems. And the fact that it was state-of-the-art made it even more desirable.

The church leadership prayed and felt we should make an offer of a specific price and not go beyond it. They had determined the offer after careful examination of the budget, and once the deal was presented, there would be no more negotiation. The bank needed to accept our terms or the deal was over. There was no investment in the outcome. Would the church love to acquire the building? Yes, but not if it was not part of God's plan.

Our pastor presented it like this: "We believe this is an opportunity to purchase a building we could definitely use. We have limited funds to offer. We have prayed, asked for wisdom, and discerned an amount and direction. Next we will present this to the bank. We will not stress over whether or not we get the building, but trust God in the process. He will provide what we need when we need it. If this is not the building for us, then we walk away knowing God has something else." It was clear from the beginning. We were not to fret over the outcome. The confidence to proceed with the purchase was based on God as the ultimate source of provision. If we went after this building with a sense of desperation, thinking we had to have it, we would be in trouble. Worry and anxiety would have been set in motion.

In the end, we did purchase the building, but the pastor was clear throughout the process that we would walk away from the deal if the offer was not accepted according to the offered terms. If we lost the purchase, it would not shake our faith or confidence in God.

What was so striking was how little our leadership was invested in the desired outcome. Because of this, they were able to approach the deal with complete openness to God's leading and directing. Consequently, worry was not part of the process.

How often do we rest in God's provision like this? Too often, we go ahead of Him, worrying the entire way. When things do not work out the way we think they should, we are easily disappointed and think He has let us down. Experience should teach us that our ideas concerning outcomes are not always best, because we do not have the full picture of what God is doing. But a turn in the road we do not want or expect can take us to an even better path.

### Trusting that God sees the full picture

Here are a few more examples to drive this point home. A mom worried that her son would not be potty-trained by the time preschool began. The preschool required all children to be potty-trained to attend. As the days went by, the mom's worry mounted because her son was not ready. She wanted him in the class. But as the start date drew nearer, her son regressed to having more accidents during the day. The more the mom pushed, the more the son regressed. She was so invested in the outcome that worry affected their relationship. She had put herself in a difficult situation. The pressure was too much, a power struggle developed, and she had to delay her son's start date. Potty-training took another six months. Once the mom resigned herself to the son's timetable, she relaxed. Some things do not happen as we plan. When we are overinvested in the outcome, stress and worry can increase.

Another parent found himself in a similar state. A dad desperately wanted his son to be accepted at an Ivy League school. This desire caused a great deal of worry among all family members—so much so that the son interviewed poorly during his meeting with the school. He was so worried he would disappoint his father that he could not relax. The father was so worried that the son would not be accepted that he did not sleep well until the letter of acceptance came. All the family members were overinvested in the outcome. Worry took over. And worry almost cost the outcome desired.

It is one thing to desire an outcome; it is another to be so invested in the outcome that you are consumed by worry. Wants and desires are fine, but when they are not realized, we need to be flexible. In the example above, the father could have encouraged his son to do his best and trust God for direction concerning the best school. He would have slept better, and the son would have interviewed with more confidence. Ultimately, we must do our best, take action toward certain outcomes, and then trust God to open or close doors. When we can do this, we rest in the outcome, knowing He is in control.

Once again, the story of Job helps reinforce the concept of not holding on to things too tightly. In the story, God had a perspective Job was incapable of having. We simply do not see the full picture of our lives. And when circumstances do not go the way we hope, and God does not explain Himself to our satisfaction, we must be careful not to give in to worry. Like Job, we must ultimately conclude that God is good and can be trusted.

**Practice problem-solving**

In a previous chapter I discussed the importance of problem-solving in order to prevent worry from taking hold. The reason for this is that pathological worry is associated with lacking the confidence that you can solve a problem, and with the belief that you do not have control over the problem-solving process. A relationship with God solves both problems. Our confidence is in Him to come through with what we need when we need it. And we are relieved by knowing He is in control of our lives.

Effective problem-solving is also dependent on your resources. If you have the means, you can usually solve a problem. Thankfully, God is a trusted resource. He is the One with answers. With Him there is always an answer.

To avoid impulsive or careless acts and address problems when they arise, problem-solving is a skill to be practiced. In the example above, our church's leadership had a problem. The church needed more space. The confidence that we could solve the space problem came from a dependence on God. We knew that if we prayed, waited on God's timing, and pursued options, the space problem would be eventually be resolved. Confidence to solve the problem was high—based not on the skilled negotiations or close relationship with the bank (although both were helpful), but rather on God's power to move on behalf of the church. Did church leaders have control over the process? Not really, but they believed that God would act on our behalf and that they were to pursue this option and rest in the outcome. Action was required to move forward. Leadership had to be diligent to explore all options, negotiate a deal, and act according to the leading of the Spirit.

The outcome of the church's building purchase arrived quickly. Most problems are not solved so quickly and require perseverance in the process. The longer it takes to solve an issue, the more tempting it is to worry. So when we take on a problem, solving it in a reasonable amount of time goes a long way to stop worry.

When you are in a position to problem-solve, experiment with a few solutions. If they do not work, try again. Do not give up until you feel you have done everything you can. Then rest in the fact that you have done your best. Related to this notion is an old saying often quoted by a friend of mine, "Act as if everything depends on you and pray as if everything depends on God."

### HOW TO BECOME A PROBLEM-SOLVER

Because problem-solving is such an important skill used to combat worry, here are guidelines to help you develop and practice this skill:

1. *Develop a positive attitude toward problems.* Have confidence that there is a solution. The times you do not see a solution, trust God. He is working behind the scenes for your good.

2. *Recognize and identify real problems.* Do not manufacture problems. Worriers imagine all the possible negative scenarios, but problem-solvers see a problem and focus on solutions. Stick to the real problem at hand.

3. *Define the problem.* Worriers are great at defining problems, but usually get stuck in the definition. They do not move beyond definitions to find solutions. Make sure you begin with a clear definition of the problem so you can move to solutions.

4. *Generate possible solutions.* Rather than getting stuck on all the possible problems that could come, focus on possible solutions. Develop a number of solutions and do not worry about whether they are all great ideas. The point is to think about options. Brainstorm. Pray. Ask God for wisdom.

5. *Make a decision as to which solution to use.* Worriers often feel they need more information than necessary to make a decision. The need for accumulating evidence can slow down the process. After you generate a number of solutions, pursue one and see what happens.

6. *Implement your solution.* Take a risk. Try something. Be proactive.

7. *Evaluate whether or not your solution is working; if not, try another one.* Take the pressure off to find something that works the first time. If you do not succeed, try another solution. The key is to be proactive looking for a way to solve the problem.

**Remember, do not avoid and suppress worried thoughts**

Another key point in cultivating a peaceful life is to change how you deal with worried thoughts. Remember, thought suppression does not work. Even though suppressing worrisome thoughts calms the body temporarily, worried thoughts keep the mind in overdrive. And those worrisome thoughts break through even more. Remember that the bottom line is that attempting to control worry through thought suppression actually maintains worry. The solution is to allow worried thoughts to come and then go. As soon as they enter your mind, remember the battle. The natural mind is at war with the mind of Christ, but you control where thoughts go when you take them captive. In order to take your thoughts captive, put on the mind of Christ. What would He think about the thought?

Think of worried thoughts like computer spam. They come into your inbox. You have no control over that. But you can delete the mail without opening it. Worried thoughts may cross your mind, but do not open them. Delete them. Then use Paul's advice from Philippians 4:8-9 (as rendered in *The Message* paraphrase):

> Summing it all up, friends, I'd say you'll do best by filling your minds and meditating on things true, noble, reputable, authentic, compelling, gracious—the best, not the worst; the beautiful, not the ugly; things to praise, not things to curse. Put into practice what you learned from me, what you heard and saw and realized. Do that, and God, who makes everything work together, will work you into his most excellent harmonies.

**Know when to ask for help**

One of the barriers to cultivating a worry-free life is to refuse to ask for help when you need it. Often, it is pride that gets in our way. As with people who refuse to ask for directions, the only thing that pride does is keep us lost. No one can solve all problems all the time. There are situations that will overwhelm even the strongest spiritual life. This is why God put us in community and thinks so highly of the body of Christ. The body needs all the parts to function well.

You may be old enough to remember a song by Bill Withers, lead singer with The Righteous Brothers. He recorded the popular song "Lean on Me." The familiar lyrics of the first two stanzas have become an anthem for our need for each other. The writer affirms that we all have sorrows and pain but if we are wise, we lean on each other. We need friends and people who are strong when we are not. As we help others in need, they, in turn, are there for us when we need a friend.

We put tremendous stress on ourselves when we try to cope with life alone. Asking for help is not a sign of weakness but of strength. It signals a willingness to do something about your weakness. We live in community, not on islands. Family and friends who support and encourage in times of difficulty are necessary help when life gets rough. I am always amazed when someone begins an e-mail to me like this: "I am so sorry to bother you, Dr. Mintle. I won't contact you again." First of all, I accept e-mail requests for help, so you are not bothering me. My purpose in being available is to help. Please do not feel guilty about asking for it. This is a good thing when you are stuck.

Now, I am not suggesting you develop an unhealthy dependence on other people. Rather, you need a healthy interdependence that comes from doing life with other people. Worry is sent packing when people support each other during times of crisis and need.

Right now I have a cousin whose daughter has experienced a number of unforeseen operations. The complications are beyond normal and are creating serious physical challenges for her. She has been in and out of the hospital for more than 40 days. No one saw this coming, and this young woman's life is on hold while the doctors figure out what is wrong and how to fix it. Like many families in similar situations, the family established an Internet site to post notes of encouragement, prayer, and support. The site provides a way for people to express their love and care. Each note is a reminder that God has not abandoned the family and is working on their behalf. The love and care of others sends worry to the back door.

We do not minimize the pain people experience when we offer

words of faith and encouragement. We mourn and grieve during difficult times with those who hurt. However, we comfort others with the same comfort we are given by God. Despite the hurt, we remain firm that nevertheless, God is with us.

The worrier allows helplessness and hopelessness to overtake his or her thinking. He or she succumbs to circumstances and limits God in the middle of them. But the person of faith operates in reality, knowing the power of God to move in even the most difficult circumstances. Thus, worry is ousted by trust in God and His goodness. Fear blinds us to such trust.

## Do not recycle the past—let it go

As a family therapist, I confess this is where I get into trouble in my own life. I understand all too well the influences of the past on the present. This is not a problem in itself. It is actually necessary for me to do my job well. But when I allow the past to *dictate* what might happen in the future, then worry takes over.

I noticed this recently with my son. Like many young adults, he has changed his major a few times since beginning college. Each time this happens, he loses credits because some of them do not transfer to his new field. This latest time he changed, I worried again about the loss of credits. Why? Because it had happened before! Even though the review committee was a different group of people and his former and new majors had more similar courses than previously, I worried based on past experience. I was not accounting for the differences that the new situation presented. And even if the courses had not transferred, what did my worry accomplish? Nothing!

### *The past does not dictate the present*

In relationships, worry about the past must be balanced by the present. The past does not dictate the present, especially in God's economy. This does not mean you ignore the past. For example, if someone had a temper problem before he started dating you, pay attention to this and look for current signs of temper problems. Your decision to date this person should take into account what you see in the present as well as this person's history. This is wisdom. However, there is a fine line between knowing the past and judging people because of it. People do grow and heal and do not remain victims of the past. Leave room for possible change.

In John 8, Jesus was teaching in the temple courts. The religious scholars of the day brought Him a woman who was caught in the act of adultery. The Law of Moses commanded that the woman be stoned because of her sin. But the religious leaders wanted to test Jesus and badgered Him to give an answer as to what He would do. In a surprising twist, Jesus turns the tables, "Whoever among you is without sin, throw the first stone." Of course, no one threw anything, and eventually they all walked away. Jesus then addressed the woman. With compassion, He told her that no one was left to accuse her. More importantly, He did not condemn her but told her to leave her life of sin. Mercy was mixed with the caution to stop sinning. For her life to change, she had to turn from her sin.

When we repent, the power of Christ in us empowers us to break free from the past. But for worry to leave, there must be a change in behavior. Relapse is almost certain if a person goes back to doing the same things that caused the problem in the first place. However, when a person commits to change and behaves in new ways, worry can be set aside. Time will tell if change will be sustained. And there is grace for the journey.

### Discerning whether true change is happening

In regard to proceeding in a troubled relationship, wisdom is needed to discern true change in another. Worrying about the past serves no purpose. It is better to focus on present behavior to determine if change is real. When the change turns out to not be authentic, more wisdom is needed to decide if you should continue with the relationship, set new boundaries, or move in a different direction. And if *you* are the one who needs to change, worry less and engage more in those things that bring freedom to your life. You do control your choices. Change is sustained when we accept personal responsibility for our actions.

To give an example, a common worry about the past involves adult children of divorce. When couples divorce, the impact reaches beyond the time of the divorce and influences their children as they grow. When adults, these children often worry that when they fall in love, they will eventually be abandoned or their own marriages will end in divorce. They worry about how to choose a partner because of what they saw with their parents. They also worry about infidelity when that was a factor in their parents' divorce.

While these concerns are real, and while patterns of intimacy are learned in families, remember, you are not a victim of the past when God is in your life. It is critical to be aware of what baggage you bring to a relationship and to work on those issues, but you can change the way you deal with intimacy in relationships. Instead of worrying about the negative impact of divorce, work on losing the baggage associated with it. Again, worry does not fix anything.

The outcome of your marriage does not have to be the same as that of your parents. While divorce does have negative effects on children, it does not doom them to be adult failures. Divorce can give you a resolve to work through problems. It can help you develop new strengths and abilities.

To repeat, if the guilt of your past is leading you to worry about the present or future, you fail to recognize the power of Christ in your life. In Him, you are no longer condemned or judged. All of us fall short and sin, but because Jesus became the ultimate sacrifice for our sins. We now live under grace, not law. Therefore when we make mistakes, we are no longer condemned by the old law, but justified through Christ. So we need to drop worry about our past. It is forgiven. Live in the freedom of Christ.

### Live a centered life

For the person of faith, a centered life is about having the right priorities and believing that God is who He says He is, and does what He promises. In Matthew 6:33, Jesus provides the prescription for a centered life when He says, "Seek first his kingdom and his righteousness, and all these things will be given to you as well." The centered life is found when we seek God and His kingdom. During Jesus' ministry on earth, He announced that the kingdom of God was at hand.[3] He was speaking about Himself. His presence on earth brought the kingdom of God to those who would follow Him. His teaching revealed this kingdom to those who would listen.

In the Sermon on the Mount, Jesus outlines kingdom values in the verses known as the Beatitudes.[4] Jesus teaches the crowd how to live so that their lives will go well. The values He emphasizes are counter to the cultural values of then and now. Kingdom living involves humility, a willingness to suffer persecution, obedience to God's commandments, right behavior versus false piety, prayer, spiritual versus material values, and being submitted to the will of God. All of this requires radical devotion and dependence on God. Our goal as kingdom followers is to live for God, not ourselves. And it is clear that God favors the humble who completely trust Him.

Jesus tells us that taking the path of materialism, wealth, and accomplishment so prevalent in the culture will not lead to a centered life. In contrast, the call to His kingdom is through repentance and humility. When we receive Jesus as Lord of our lives, the kingdom of God indwells us. We are no longer on our own, subject to worry and hopelessness, but members of a new kingdom that empowers us though surrender to God.

As we seek this kingdom and God's righteousness, there is no need to worry, because God will meet our basic needs. When we are in tune with God's agenda for our lives, He assures us that He will ultimately fulfill His purposes and promises. As we fully grasp the idea that God is ultimately responsible for the outcome of a life surrendered to Him, we can rest in this assurance. God is in control.

Furthermore, Jesus adds in verse 34 of Matthew 6 that worry does not add a moment to our lives. Jesus did not need modern stress research to know that worry shortens lives and creates damage to the physical body. As our Creator, He knows the impact of worry on the bodies He designed! His directive to let tomorrow take care of itself is meant for our self-care. A life centered on God is a life that is not anxious about the future.

Daily, God asks us to bring our needs to Him in prayer and He will meet them. He may not meet them in the time and way we have in mind, but He will meet them according to His greater knowledge of us.

As the Psalms declare, God is not bothered by our conversations of pain and angst. Our emotions run full circle—happy to sad, elated to discouraged, and so on. Whatever our state, we can share our reality with God. In difficult times, He will strengthen us to not be moved by circumstances. Happy are those who put their trust in God. A life centered in God is a worry-free life.

### The way to a centered life

When I first read the book of Ecclesiastes, I found it depressing. Its heavy theme of despair left me feeling defeated. Here was the wisest and most powerful man of his day declaring life to be meaningless. Everything in me wanted to provide therapy for this anonymous author, the Teacher. He had riches, power, and fame, yet his conclusions about life make you want to open the freezer and down a gallon of ice cream! Eat, drink, and be merry—tomorrow we die. Bad things happen to good people. No matter what, life turns out poorly.

The more I read, the more I thought this guy needed a medication evaluation, maybe an antidepressant! In Ecclesiastes, nothing seems to work out. You can accumulate wealth and power, but life is still meaningless. All is vanity! Then I realized that is the point. When we live our lives apart from God, no amount of riches or excess brings meaning or contentment. And in fact, such abundance often brings anxiety and worry. In a day when we are told that wealth, fame, and power end worry, Ecclesiastes reminds us that having it all is *not* the antidote.

The Teacher's final wisdom is offered at the end of the book. He concludes, fear God and keep His commandments. God will judge everything, good and evil.[5] In the end, nothing satisfies but God. After several chapters of angst, wisdom declares that God is the source of true contentment.

### Seek wisdom

Wisdom has been desired since the beginning of creation. When God created Adam and Eve and placed them in the Garden, Satan tempted Eve to eat fruit from the tree God had restricted. The passage in Genesis 3:6 reads, "When the woman saw that the fruit of the tree was good for food and pleasing to the eye, *and also desirable for gaining wisdom*, she took some and ate it. She also gave some to her husband, who was with her, and he ate it." Notice the phrase, "and also desirable for gaining wisdom." The first temptation involved a desire for wisdom. Eve had the source of all wisdom at her side daily. She walked and talked with God. His wisdom was always available.

The temptation posed by the serpent was to be like God or on an even level with Him. This desire to be elevated to God's status is what caused Satan to be ousted from heaven. Now he is looking for partners in his quest to overthrow God. When Eve listened to the serpent instead of God, she sinned. Her decision to go her own way instead of His way led to a change in relationship and history. Wisdom is not gained by disobedience to God's instruction. There is no wisdom in elevating ourselves above God. In fact, doing so gives birth to worry.

### Only true wisdom eliminates worry

Wisdom apart from God is not true wisdom. He is wisdom. When His wisdom intersects with our daily life, it takes away worry and rids us of anxiety. Thus, gaining wisdom is something to be desired. Proverbs 4:5-9 tells us,

> Get wisdom, get understanding; do not forget my words or swerve from them.
>
> Do not forsake wisdom, and she will protect you; love her, and she will watch over you.
>
> Wisdom is supreme; therefore get wisdom. Though it cost all you have, get understanding.
>
> Esteem her, and she will exalt you; embrace her, and she will honor you.
>
> She will set a garland of grace on your head and present you with a crown of splendor.

King Solomon understood the importance of asking for wisdom. When he became the king of God's chosen people following his father David's rule, he realized the magnitude of the job he had inherited. Being king was a daunting task. In 1 Kings 3:7-10, he told God that he was too young, did not know the ropes, and was responsible for a people too numerous to count. Most of us would agree that he sounds a bit overwhelmed. Then, he petitioned God for a listening heart needed to lead the people well and a discerning spirit to distinguish between good and evil. He recognized his need for godly wisdom and added that on his own he could not do the job.

### God will respond to our request

God responded to Solomon's request for wisdom with sheer delight. He not only gave the wisdom requested, but also told Solomon that there never was or will be anyone like him in regards to wisdom. Then God threw in a bonus reward of wealth and glory. Finally, God made it clear to Solomon that if he kept His commandments, long life would also be granted. All of this came from Solomon asking for wisdom to rule wisely.

When we ask for wisdom, according to James 1:5, God is ready to supply an ample amount: "If any of you lacks wisdom, he should ask God, who gives *generously* to all without finding fault, and it will be given to him." James discusses this request in the context of living a holy life in unconditional obedience to God. He urges us to patiently endure trials, knowing that the testing of our faith makes us strong. To help us along the way, God says He will give us wisdom to guide us. So rather than worry when trials come, we are to ask God for wisdom in the middle of the trial. He promises to liberally provide the wisdom we need during those times of discouragement and situations that could be anxiety-producing.

A powerful example of this can be seen in the lives of Jesus' disciples. When He prepared them to go out and be His witnesses, He let them know they would face persecution. However, during those times, they would not be operating in their own strength. In Matthew 10:19, Jesus urged them to be confident during persecution because He would give them the words to say when they were arrested and brought to trial. In Luke, Jesus gave a similar directive—they were not to worry about how they would defend themselves when brought before synagogues, rulers, and authorities to be tried. He would be their defense.

In Luke 21:14, Jesus urged the disciples to *make up their minds* not to worry. This implied taking charge of their thoughts and allowing the Holy Spirit to guide their words. In other words, they would have the wisdom needed to deal with difficult situations. The same is true today. Do not worry. Trust God to give you the wisdom you need when you need it.

### Focus on God's wisdom

Because we live in a time when there is much we could worry about, the words of the psalmist are especially pertinent. David could have easily worried, given all the troubles he faced. But time and again, he turned his thoughts to the goodness of God. When we read David's desperate cries to the Lord and hear the rawness of his emotions, we know his human heart was frequently burdened. Regularly, he faced difficult circumstances. He struggled with rejection, disappointment, betrayal, and a multitude of emotions that can easily lead to worry and anxious living. But David chose to depend on God and His wisdom. The result was total surrender to God, as summed up in Psalm 31:15: "My times are in your hands." Oh, if we could all rest in that truth!

There are times in our lives when we need to stop trying to figure it all out and trust that our lives are in God's hands. We do not have the full story of our lives or know what He is doing behind the scenes. What does not make sense to us makes perfect sense to Him. If we trust Him, are obedient to His words, and ask for wisdom, worry has to leave. Rest and peace are worry's replacements. So no matter your troubles or circumstances, with God's help, say goodbye to worry and do not invite it back.

## Worry-Free Exercise

**BODY:**

Practice living a centered life. Keep God in the forefront, spend time in prayer, and ask liberally for wisdom.

**SOUL:**

Become a problem-solver. Take any situation that has you worried and apply the problem-solving guidelines to it.

**SPIRIT:**

If you desire wisdom, ask God for it. Pray according to Scripture. Meditate on Proverbs 3:13-20. Be obedient to God's commands, fear Him, and ask for what you need. Be bold in your request and believe He will do what He says.

*Blessed is the man who finds wisdom, the man who gains understanding, for she is more profitable than silver and yields better returns than gold. She is more precious than rubies; nothing you desire can compare with her. Long life is in her right hand; in her left hand are riches and honor. Her ways are pleasant ways, and all her paths are peace. She is a tree of life to those who embrace her; those who lay hold of her will be blessed.*

*By wisdom the LORD laid the earth's foundations, by understanding he set the heavens in place; by his knowledge the deeps were divided, and the clouds let drop the dew.*

*My son, preserve sound judgment and discernment, do not let them out of your sight; they will be life for you, an ornament to grace your neck. Then you will go on your way in safety, and your foot will not stumble.*

# Epilogue

admit it. Writing this book has deeply challenged me. Worry has been a part of my life for so many years…causing sleepless nights and zapping me of needed energy. While I am not completely worry-free, I am working on it every day. Daily, I take thoughts captive and remind myself to trust God and believe His promises. I hope that you will join me in this journey.

Please do not feel condemned because you struggle with worry or anxiety. There is grace. Grace is what nudges us to be more like Christ. We then respond to that grace by asking God to change us through the power of His Spirit working in us. We accomplish such change through the working of this grace. Ask God to help you leave worry at the door-step. Humbly admit your weakness and accept His power to change you.

During the writing of this book, I encountered circumstances that could have created significant worry. I spent many nights crying out to God and taking my cares to the foot of the cross. I echo the sentiment of Psalm 124: "If the LORD had not been on our side…" But He *is* by my side, and by yours as well. He calls you to come to Him, you who are weary and burdened, and He will give you rest.

I encourage you to go through the chapters of this book and work on the parts that keep worry alive and working in your life. Hold on to hope, and do your best to trust God. During those times of struggle, ask Him to help your unbelief. Jesus showed great compassion for those who cried out to Him in this regard.

He knows your situation (Psalm 56:8) and cares about your trouble (Psalm 103:13-14). Best of all, He can change you and your situation

(Ephesians 3:20). But Galatians 3:3 reminds us that change does not come through self-effort. Allow God to work on you and see what He does in this area of worry. I would love to hear about your progress and welcome your feedback. Please feel free to e-mail me or post on my website or Facebook page.

The only certainty we have in life is God. To quote the cliché, life is not easy. But God proclaims that His yoke is easy and His burden is light. Those words soar in song during my yearly attendance of one of the most beautiful and inspiring pieces of music ever performed—Handel's *Messiah*. The truth of those words is powerful.

God invites us to cast our cares on Him. Every day, rehearse His goodness, brings those worries to Him, and let them go. Accept His grace. Walk in the confidence that He is in control and working all things together for your good. He knows your heart and will bring you peace and rest.

If we want to model our lives after Christ, we only have to look at the Garden of Gethsemane. Knowing He would soon be put to death, Jesus agonized with tears, pleading, intercession, and prayers and prostrated Himself before the Father. Everything had been tried. The end was near, and in Matthew 26:39 He concluded with this: "Yet not as I will, but as you will."

When worry comes knocking at your door, do not invite it in. Instead, pray the prayer of Jesus: "Not as I will, but as You will. I do not think I can handle it. I feel overwhelmed, but You are Almighty God and I can rest in You. Take it, do what You choose when You choose to do it. You are my Father and I am Your child." Surrender to the One who loves you, and allow Him to shoulder the burdens of this life. Exchange your worry for His rest.

*Grace and peace be yours in abundance through the knowledge*
*of God and of Jesus our Lord. His divine power has given*
*us everything we need for life and godliness through our*
*knowledge of him who called us by his own glory and goodness.*

—2 PETER 1:2-3

# Meditation Scriptures

## Worry

*Deuteronomy 31:8*

> The LORD himself goes before you and will be with you; he will never leave you nor forsake you. Do not be afraid; do not be discouraged.

*Psalm 9:10*

> Those who know your name will trust in you, for you, LORD, have never forsaken those who seek you.

*Psalm 23:1-6*

> The LORD is my shepherd, I shall not be in want. He makes me lie down in green pastures, he leads me beside quiet waters, he restores my soul. He guides me in paths of righteousness for his name's sake. Even though I walk through the valley of the shadow of death, I will fear no evil, for you are with me; your rod and your staff, they comfort me. You prepare a table before me in the presence of my enemies. You anoint my head with oil; my cup overflows. Surely goodness and love will follow me all the days of my life, and I will dwell in the house of the LORD forever.

*Psalm 32:7*

> You are my hiding place; you will protect me from trouble and surround me with songs of deliverance. Selah.

*Psalm 34:4*

> I sought the LORD, and he heard me, and delivered me from all my fears (NKJV).

*Psalm 42:5*

Why are you downcast, O my soul? Why so disturbed within me? Put your hope in God, for I will yet praise him, my Savior and my God.

*Psalm 46:1*

God is our refuge and strength, an ever-present help in trouble.

*Psalm 50:15*

Call upon me in the day of trouble; I will deliver you, and you will honor me.

*Psalm 54:4*

Surely God is my help; the LORD is the one who sustains me.

*Psalm 56:3*

When I am afraid, I will trust in you.

*Psalm 94:19*

When anxiety was great within me, your consolation brought joy to my soul.

*Psalm 112:7-8*

He will have no fear of bad news; his heart is steadfast, trusting in the LORD. His heart is secure, he will have no fear; in the end he will look in triumph on his foes.

*Psalm 124:8*

Our help is in the name of the LORD, the Maker of heaven and earth.

*Psalm 139:23*

Search me, O God, and know my heart; test me and know my anxious thoughts.

*Proverbs 12:25*

An anxious heart weighs a man down, but a kind word cheers him up.

### Matthew 6:25-26

Do not worry about your life, what you will eat or drink; or about your body, what you will wear. Is not life more important than food, and the body more important than clothes? Look at the birds of the air; they do not sow or reap or store away in barns, and yet your heavenly Father feeds them. Are you not much more valuable than they? Who of you by worrying can add a single hour to his life?

### Matthew 6:28-34

Why do you worry about clothes? See how the lilies of the field grow. They do not labor or spin. Yet I tell you that not even Solomon in all his splendor was dressed like one of these. If that is how God clothes the grass of the field, which is here today and tomorrow is thrown into the fire, will he not much more clothe you, O you of little faith? So do not worry, saying, "What shall we eat?" or "What shall we drink?" or "What shall we wear?" For the pagans run after all these things, and your heavenly Father knows that you need them. But seek first his kingdom and his righteousness, and all these things will be given to you as well. Therefore do not worry about tomorrow, for tomorrow will worry about itself. Each day has enough trouble of its own.

### Matthew 11:28

Come to me, all you who are weary and burdened, and I will give you rest.

### Mark 11:23

I tell you the truth, if anyone says to this mountain, "Go, throw yourself into the sea," and does not doubt in his heart but believes that what he says will happen, it will be done for him.

### Luke 12:25-27

Who of you by worrying can add a single hour to his life? Since you cannot do this very little thing, why do you worry about the rest? Consider how the lilies grow. They do not labor or spin. Yet I tell you, not even Solomon in all his splendor was dressed like one of these.

*Romans 12:2*

Do not conform any longer to the pattern of this world, but be transformed by the renewing of your mind. Then you will be able to test and approve what God's will is—his good, pleasing and perfect will.

*2 Corinthians 10:4-5*

The weapons we fight with are not the weapons of the world. On the contrary, they have divine power to demolish strongholds. We demolish arguments and every pretension that sets itself up against the knowledge of God, and we take captive every thought to make it obedient to Christ.

*2 Corinthians 12:9*

He said to me, "My grace is sufficient for you, for my power is made perfect in weakness." Therefore I will boast all the more gladly about my weaknesses, so that Christ's power may rest on me.

*Philippians 4:6-7*

Do not be anxious about anything, but in everything, by prayer and petition, with thanksgiving, present your requests to God. And the peace of God, which transcends all understanding, will guard your hearts and your minds in Christ Jesus.

*Philippians 4:19*

My God will meet all your needs according to his glorious riches in Christ Jesus.

*1 Peter 5:6-7*

Humble yourselves, therefore, under God's mighty hand, that he may lift you up in due time. Cast all your anxiety on him because he cares for you.

*1 John 4:18-19*

There is no fear in love. But perfect love drives out fear, because fear has to do with punishment. The one who fears is not made perfect in love. We love because he first loved us.

## Contentment

*Psalm 4:8*

I will lie down and sleep in peace, for you alone, O LORD, make me dwell in safety.

*Psalm 8:4*

What is man that you are mindful of him, the son of man that you care for him?

*Psalm 28:7*

The LORD is my strength and my shield; my heart trusts in him, and I am helped. My heart leaps for joy and I will give thanks to him in song.

*Psalm 37:7*

Quiet down before God, be prayerful before him. Don't bother with those who climb the ladder, who elbow their way to the top (MSG).

*Psalm 46:10*

Be still, and know that I am God: I will be exalted among the nations, I will be exalted in the earth.

*Psalm 4:4-5*

Complain if you must, but don't lash out. Keep your mouth shut, and let your heart do the talking. Build your case before God and wait for his verdict (MSG).

*Matthew 11:28-30*

Come to me, all you who are weary and burdened, and I will give you rest. Take my yoke upon you and learn from me, for I am gentle and humble in heart, and you will find rest for your souls. For my yoke is easy and my burden is light.

*2 Corinthians 3:5*

Not that we are competent in ourselves to claim anything for ourselves, but our competence comes from God.

*2 Corinthians 10:4-5*

The weapons we fight with are not the weapons of the world. On the contrary, they have divine power to demolish strongholds. We demolish arguments and every pretension that sets itself up against the knowledge of God, and we take captive every thought to make it obedient to Christ.

*2 Corinthians 12:9*

He said to me, "My grace is sufficient for you, for my power is made perfect in weakness." Therefore I will boast all the more gladly about my weaknesses, so that Christ's power may rest on me.

*Philippians 4:7*

The peace of God, which transcends all understanding, will guard your hearts and your minds in Christ Jesus.

*Philippians 4:11-13*

I am not saying this because I am in need, for I have learned to be content whatever the circumstances. I know what it is to be in need, and I know what it is to have plenty. I have learned the secret of being content in any and every situation, whether well fed or hungry, whether living in plenty or in want. I can do everything through him who gives me strength.

*Philippians 4:19*

My God will meet all your needs according to his glorious riches in Christ Jesus.

*1 Timothy 6:6-10*

Godliness with contentment is great gain. For we brought nothing into the world, and we can take nothing out of it. But if we have food and clothing, we will be content with that. People who want to get rich fall into temptation and a trap and into many foolish and harmful desires that plunge men into ruin and destruction. For the love of money is a root of all kinds of evil. Some people, eager for money, have wandered from the faith and pierced themselves with many griefs.

*1 Peter 1:3*

Praise be to the God and Father of our Lord Jesus Christ! In his great mercy he has given us new birth into a living hope through the resurrection of Jesus Christ from the dead.

## Wisdom

*Proverbs 1:7*

The fear of the LORD is the beginning of knowledge, but fools despise wisdom and discipline.

*Proverbs 2:6*

The LORD gives wisdom, and from his mouth come knowledge and understanding.

*Proverbs 2:12*

Wisdom will save you from the ways of wicked men, from men whose words are perverse.

*Proverbs 3:5*

Trust in the LORD with all your heart and lean not on your own understanding; in all your ways acknowledge him, and he will make your paths straight. Do not be wise in your own eyes; fear the LORD and shun evil. This will bring health to your body and nourishment to your bones.

*Proverbs 3:13-20*

Blessed is the man who finds wisdom, the man who gains understanding, for she is more profitable than silver and yields better returns than gold. She is more precious than rubies; nothing you desire can compare with her. Long life is in her right hand; in her left hand are riches and honor. Her ways are pleasant ways, and all her paths are peace. She is a tree of life to those who embrace her; those who lay hold of her will be blessed.

By wisdom the LORD laid the earth's foundations, by understanding he set the heavens in place; by his knowledge the deeps were divided, and the clouds let drop the dew.

My son, preserve sound judgment and discernment, do not let them out of your sight; they will be life for you, an ornament to grace your neck. Then you will go on your way in safety, and your foot will not stumble.

### Proverbs 9:9-12

The fear of the LORD is the beginning of wisdom, and knowledge of the Holy One is understanding. For through me your days will be many, and years will be added to your life. If you are wise, your wisdom will reward you; if you are a mocker, you alone will suffer.

### Proverbs 17:24

A discerning man keeps wisdom in view, but a fool's eyes wander to the ends of the earth.

### James 1:5-6

If any of you lacks wisdom, he should ask God, who gives generously to all without finding fault, and it will be given to him. But when he asks, he must believe and not doubt, because he who doubts is like a wave of the sea, blown and tossed by the wind.

### James 3:17

The wisdom that comes from heaven is first of all pure; then peace-loving, considerate, submissive, full of mercy and good fruit, impartial and sincere.

# Notes

### Chapter 1—Everyone Worries, Don't They?

1. *Webster's 1828 Dictionary*, s.v. "worry."

2. Edward Hallowell, "Fighting life's 'What Ifs': Why we worry, fuss and fret more than we need to," *Psychology Today*, November 1997, www.psychologytoday.com/articles/199711/fighting-lifes-what-ifs.

### Chapter 2—Life, Difficult Times, and the Nightly News

1. Melinda Beck, "When Fretting is in your DNA: Overcoming the worry gene," *Wall Street Journal*, January 15, 2008, online edition, http://online.wsj.com/article/SB120035992325490045.html, accessed March 10, 2010.

2. Stefan Hofmann et al., "The Worried Mind: Autonomic and Prefrontal Activation During Worrying," *Emotion* 5, no. 4 (2005): 464.

3. Tina Lonsdorf et al., "Genetic Gating of Human Fear Learning and Extinction: Possible Implications for Gene-Environment Interaction in Anxiety Disorder," *Psychological Science* 20, no. 2 (2009): http://pss.sagepub.com/content/20/2/198.

### Chapter 3—Confessions of Worriers: Why We Do It

1. Thomas Borkovec, Holly Hazlett-Stevens, and M.L. Diaz, "The Role of Positive Beliefs About Worry in Generalized Anxiety Disorders and its Treatment," *Clinical Psychology and Psychotherapy* 6 (1999): 126-138.

### Chapter 4—Worried Sick: The Physical Toll of Worry

1. J.M. Stavosky and T.D. Borkovec, "The Phenomenon of Worry: Theory, Research, Treatment and its Implications for Women," *Women and Therapy* 6, (1988): 77-95.

2. Stavosky and Borkovec, 87.

3. W.R. Gove, "Mental Illness and Psychiatric Treatment Among Women," *Psychology of Women Quarterly* 4 (1980): 345-362.

4. Melisa Robichaud, Michel Dugas, and Michael Conway, "Gender Differences in Worry and Associated Cognitive-Behavioral Variables," *Journal of Anxiety Disorders* 17, no. 5 (2003): 501-516.

5. Wendy-Jo Wood, Michael Conway, and Michel Dugas, "Perceived Worry and Gender Differences: Do People Perceive Women as Worrying More than Men?" (presented at the annual convention of the Canadian Psychological Association, Ottawa, Ontario, June 2000).

6. Robichaud et al.: 501-516.

7. Holly Hazlett-Stevens, *Women Who Worry Too Much* (Oakland, California: New Harbinger Publications, 2005), 9-10.

8. WebMD, "How worry affects your body," www.webmd.com/balance/how-worrying-affects-your-body?page=2.

9. Jos Brosschot, William Gerin, and Julian F. Thayer, "The Perseverative Cognition Hypothesis: A Review of Worry, Prolonged Stress-Related Physiological Activation, and Health," *Journal of Psychosomatic Research* 60, no.2 (2006): 113-124.

10. Brosschot et al.: 113-124.

11. S.R. Vrana, B.N. Cuthbert, and P.J. Lang, "Fear imagery and text processing," *Psychophysiology* 23 (1986): 247-253.

12. Suzanne Pieper, Jos Brosschot, Rien van der Leeden, and Julian Thayer, "Cardiac Effects of Momentary Assessed Worry Episodes and Stressful events," *Psychosomatic Medicine* 69 (2007), www.psychosomaticmedicine.org/cgi/content/full/69/9/901?ck=nck.

13. Laura Kubzansky et al., "Is Worrying Bad for Your Heart? A Prospective Study of Worry and Coronary Heart Disease in the Normative Aging Study," *Circulation* 95, no. 4 (1997): 818-824.

14. Daniel Mroczek, Avron Spiro III, and Nicholas Turiano, "Do Health Behaviors Explain the Effect of Neuroticism on Mortality? Longitudinal Findings from the VA Normative Aging Study," *Journal of Research in Personality* 43, no. 4 (2009): 653.

15. Thomas D. Borkovec and S. Hu, "The Effect of Worry on Cardiovascular Response to Phobic Imagery," *Behaviour Research and Therapy* 28 (1990): 69-73.

16. Ellen Michaud, *Sleep to be Sexy, Smart and Slim* (Pleasantville, NY: Readers' Digest Books, 2008).

17. Maria Essig, "Insomnia: Improving Your Sleep," WebMD 2010, www.webmd.com/sleep-disorders/how-to-set-up-a-healthy-sleep-environment, accessed March 17, 2010.

18. Andrew Parrott and N.J. Garnham, "Comparative Mood States and Cognitive Skills of Cigarette Smokers, Deprived Smokers and Nonsmokers," *Human Psychopharmacology* 13 (1998): 367-376.

19. John Hughes, "Tobacco Withdrawal in Self-Quitters," *Journal of Consulting and Clinical Psychology* 60 (1992): 689-697.

20. American Psychiatric Association, *Diagnostic and Statistical Manual of Mental Disorders: DSM-IV-TR* (Washington, DC: American Psychiatric Association, 2000), 433-436.

**Chapter 5—Worry Began in a Garden: The Spiritual Roots of Worry**

1. Eugene Peterson, *A Long Obedience in the Same Direction* (Downers Grove, IL: Intervarsity Press, 2000), 86-87.

2. The New Testament Greek Lexicon, www.studylight.org/lex/grk/view.cgi?number=3309.

3. Andrew Newberg et al. "Cerebral blood flow during meditative prayer: Preliminary findings and methodological issues," *Perceptual and Motor Skills* 97 (2003): 625-630.

4. *Matthew Henry's Commentary in the Whole Bible, Complete and Unabridged in One Volume* (Chicago: Moody Press, 1966), Psalm 55:22.

**Chapter 6—What to Do with Worried Thoughts**

1. Siamek Khodarahimi and Nnamdi Pole, "Cognitive Behavior Therapy and Worry Reduction in an Outpatient with Generalized Anxiety Disorder," *Clinical Psychology and Psychotherapy* 6 (2009): 297.

2. Daniel Wegner et al., "Paradoxical Effects of Thought Suppression," *Journal of Personality and Social Psychology* 53, no. 1 (July 1987): 5-13.

## Chapter 7—Health Worries

1. Luanne Bradley, "Toxic Nail Salons: Why Your Nail Polish Color Could be the Next Agent Orange," Personal Health AlterNet, April 21, 2010, www.alternet.org/health/146547/toxic_nail_salons:_why_your_nail_polish_color_could_be_the_next_agent_orange/.

2. Bradley.

3. Anahad O'Connor, "The Claim: Salons' UV Nail Lights can Cause Skin Cancer," *New York Times Online*, August 2, 2010, www.nytimes.com/2010/08/03/health/03real.html.

4. Robert Baan et al., "Carcinogenicity of some aromatic amines, organic dyes, and related exposures," *Lancet Oncology* 9, no. 4 (2008 ): 322-323.

5. Yawei Zhang et al., "Personal hair dye use may increase the risk of non-Hodgkin lymphoma subtypes," *American Journal of Epidemiology* 167, no. 11 (2008): 1321-1331.

6. American Cancer Society, "Learn About Cancer," www.cancer.org/Cancer/CancerCauses/OtherCarcinogens/MedicalTreatments/radiation-exposure-and-cancer.

7. Anna Short, "US infertility statistics," http://ezinearticles.com/?US-Infertility-Statistics&id=4651989, accessed September 11, 2010.

## Chapter 8—Job Worries

1. Northwestern National Life survey, " Employee burnout: America's newest epidemic," (Minneapolis, MN: Northwestern National Life Insurance Company, 1991).

2. Bureau of Labor Statistics, " Tabular data, 1992-96: Number and percentage distribution of non-fatal occupational injuries and illnesses involving days away from work, by nature of injury or illness and number of days away from work," 1996, accessed 1998.

3. Daniel Mroczek, Avron Spiro III, and Nicholas A. Turiano, "Do Health Behaviors Explain the Effect of Neuroticism on Mortality? Longitudinal Findings from the VA Normative Aging Study," *Journal of Research in Personality* 43, no. 4 (2009): 653.

4. Jeffrey Edwards, "Person-Job Fit: A Conceptual Integration, Literature Review, and Methodological Critique," in C.L. Cooper and I.T. Robertson, eds., *International Review of Industrial and Organizational Psychology* (New York: Wiley, 1991), vol.6, 283-357.

5. Ed Diener, John Helliwell, and Daniel Kahneman, *International Differences in Well-Being* ( New York: Oxford University Press, 2010), 400-402.

6. Avue Technologies Corporation, "Taking the Helm: Attracting the Next Generation of Federal Leaders," copyright 2010 by the Senior Executives Association and Avue Technologies Corporation, www.seniorexecs.org/fileadmin/user_upload/Professional_Development/Research/Taking_the_Helm/Executive_Summary.pdf, accessed June 14, 2010.

## Chapter 9—Money Worries

1. Pew Research Center, "Are We Happy Yet?" February 6, 2006, http://pewresearch.org/pubs/301/are-we-happy-yet, survey data Oct18-Nov 9, 2006, accessed June 17, 2010.

2. Reader's Digest survey, "Poll: Money worries world's greatest cause of stress," September 30, 2009, www.cnn.com/2009/WORLD/americas/09/30/stress.survey.money/index.html, accessed June 17, 2010.

3. Frank Newport, Gallup poll, "Worries about money peak with forty-somethings," February 27, 2009, www.gallup.com/poll/116131/worry-money-peaks-forty-somethings.aspx.

4. Newport.

5. Karen Pine, *Sheconomics* (Terra Alta, WV: Headline Book Publisher, 2009).

6. User Interface Engineering, "What causes customers to buy on impulse?" E-commerce white paper, www.uie.com/publications/whitepapers/ImpulseBuying.pdf, accessed July 2, 2010.

7. Annette Elton, "I'll take that, too: Increasing impulse buys," www.giftshopmag.com/2008/spring/unique_giftware/increasing_impulse_buys.

8. Rosemary Black, "The power of money: Just touching and thinking about it can make us feel better, research finds," *New York Daily News*, August 6, 2009 www.nydailynews.com/lifestyle/health/2009/07/28/2009-07-28_the_power_of_money_just_touching_and_thinking_about_it_can_make_us_feel_better_r.html, accessed July 6, 2010.

9. ScienceDaily. "University of Rochester: Achieving Fame, Wealth and Beauty Are Psychological Dead Ends, Study Says," 2009, May 19, www.sciencedaily.com /releases/2009/05/090514111402 .htm, accessed August 19, 2010.

**Chapter 11—How to Live in the Moment**

1. See Matthew 6:34.

2. See 2 Corinthians 4:4; Romans 1:28.

3. See Romans 7:18.

4. Matthew 11:28.

5. Meher McArthur, *Reading Buddhist Art: An Illustrated Guide to Buddhist Signs and Symbols* (New York: Thames & Hudson, 2004), 149.

6. See 1 Corinthians 3:18-20 and Colossians 1:9-10.

7. See Psalm 8:4.

8. See, respectively, Romans 12:2, Matthew 22:37, and Hebrews 10:16.

9. Psalm 46:10 NASB.

**Chapter 12—Practical Help to Send Worry Packing**

1. Deuteronomy 31:8.

**Chapter 14—Cultivate a Worry-Free Life**

1. John 16:33.

2. John 14:1.

3. See Mark 1:15.

4. See Matthew 5:1-12.

5. See Ecclesiastes 12:13-14.

## About Dr. Linda Mintle

It is often said that being with Dr. Linda is like having coffee with a friend. She makes the complicated issues of relationships and mental health easy to understand and applicable to everyday living. The ease she has with people, coupled with her clinical training and experience, makes her a sought-after speaker on college campuses, at conferences, and at special events. Whether she is doing a TV skit with Tim Conway or discussing teen violence with Queen Latifah, Dr. Linda entertains, educates, and brings common sense along with her clinical training.

Dr. Linda is a licensed marriage and family therapist and clinical social worker, an approved supervisor for the American Association for Marriage and Family Therapy, and a diplomate in social work. She is also Assistant Professor of Clinical Pediatrics, Department of Pediatrics, at Eastern Virginia Medical School, a media personality, and a consultant/contributor for national news. She earned her PhD in Urban Health and Clinical Psychology from Old Dominion University and is now a national speaker and bestselling author, with 16 book titles currently published. Known for her humor and practical advice, Dr. Linda knows how to motivate her audience to positive life change.

To book Dr. Linda for speaking, contact:

Ambassador Speakers Bureau
PO Box 50358, Nashville, TN 37205
(615) 370-4700

E-mail: info@AmbassadorSpeakers.com

For more help or information regarding Dr. Linda, visit her Web site at www.drlindahelps.com and her Facebook page, "Dr. Linda Mintle, Author and Speaker."

# Also by Dr. Linda Mintle

**I Love My Mother, But...**
*Practical Help to Get the Most Out of Your Relationship*

Whether your mom did a great job raising you or left a lot to be desired as a parent, you always have issues to work out between the two of you. Like many grown daughters, you probably struggle to find balance and perspective with your mother.

With real-life stories and biblical insight, family life expert Dr. Linda Mintle shows how you can build your connection with your mother as you

- deal with unrealistic expectations

- break old patterns and learn better ways to deal with conflict

- let go of guilt and shame and find peace and emotional healing

Whatever your mom is like, whatever she does or doesn't do, you can learn new ways to approach her. In the process, you will understand yourself and her better...and grow and move forward into new possibilities.

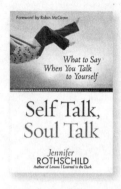

**Self Talk, Soul Talk**

What to Say When You Talk to Yourself

*Jennifer Rothschild*

Have you ever noticed the things you silently tell yourself—and believe? *"I could never do that." "They don't like me." "I am such an idiot!"*

Phrases like these endlessly flow through your mind and pool in the depths of your soul. How can you replace these lies with truth? Popular author and Women of Faith speaker Jennifer Rothschild shows how you can stop the flood of negative self-talk and fill your mind with life-giving biblical principles.

Discover what David the psalmist, Deborah the prophet, and other biblical personalities said to themselves, and you'll experience new freedom and vitality as you dive into a refreshing stream of truthful soul-talk.

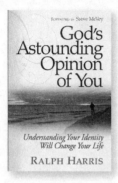

**God's Astounding Opinion of You**
Understanding Your Identity Will
Change Your Life
*Ralph Harris*

Do you know that God's view of you is much greater than your own? Ralph Harris, founder and President of LifeCourse Ministries, leads you to embrace the Scriptures' truth about what God thinks of you—that you are special to Him, blameless, pure, and lovable.

With clear and simple explanations and examples, this resource will help you turn toward the love affair with God you were created for…a relationship in which you

- exchange fear and obligation for delight and devotion

- recognize the remarkable role and strength of the Holy Spirit in your daily life

- view your status as a *new creation* as the "new normal"— and live accordingly!

## How to Get Past Disappointment
Finding Hope
*Michelle McKinney Hammond*

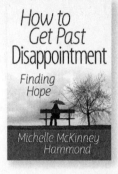

Mistakes, regrets, and failures. Love lost. Dreams delayed. Everyone experiences disappointments. But are you hung up on…trapped by…disappointment in your life?

Bestselling author Michelle McKinney Hammond tells you how's she's been there as she explores the Bible's "woman at the well" story from John chapter 4. She shows how Jesus' gentle but firm touch can open up the deepest parts of your heart and free you from the disappointment trap.

As an added bonus, Michelle includes insightful questions and uplifting affirmations to help you live the life God wants you to have.

## How to Get Past Disappointment DVD
Six Powerful Sessions for Finding Hope

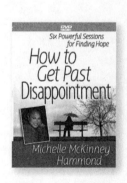

In six powerful 30-minute sessions, Michelle helps you ask yourself the same questions Jesus asks:

1. Who Am I?

2. Who Is He, and What Is He to You?

3. What Do You Really Want?

4. What Is True Worship?

5. What Is True Nourishment?

6. What Is Your Life Reflecting?

Like the woman at the well, you can look away from yourself, look toward the Son of God…and move forward in joy and freedom.

*Helpful leader's guide included. Perfect for small-group or church curriculum.*

**Taking Out Your Emotional Trash**
Face Your Feelings and Build Healthy
Relationships
*Georgia Shaffer*

Do you want more energy, more peace, more happiness? Christian psychologist Georgia Shaffer offers a proven "toss and recycle" program to help you evaluate your emotions, keep the life-affirming ones, and discard the ones that hinder healthy relationships. Step-by-step you'll discover how to...

- reduce destructive anxiety, fear, guilt, and shame

- eliminate persistent, toxic emotions

- experience greater intimacy in relationships

- handle life's ups and downs more easily

- introduce more hope and joy into your life

Through real-life stories, insightful questions, and wisdom from God's Word, you'll discover transforming truths that will help you be free to be who you are—loved, talented, valued, and forgiven.

To learn more about other Harvest House books
or to read sample chapters, log on to our website:

**www.harvesthousepublishers.com**

HARVEST HOUSE PUBLISHERS

EUGENE, OREGON